The World's Regions and Weather

Linking Fiction to Nonfiction

PHYLLIS J. PERRY

D1737696

TEACHER IDEAS PRESS
A Division of
Libraries Unlimited, Inc.
Englewood, Colorado
1996

TEACHER IDEAS PRESS
A Division of Libraries Unlimited, Inc.
P.O. Box 6633
Englewood, CO 80155-6633
1-800-237-6124

Production Editor: Jason Cook
Copy Editor: D. Aviva Rothschild
Layout and Interior Design: Kay Minnis

Library of Congress Cataloging-in-Publication Data

Perry, Phyllis Jean.
    The world's regions and weather : linking fiction to nonfiction /
Phyllis J. Perry.
        xvi, 157 p. 22x28 cm. -- (Literature bridges to science)
        Includes index.
        ISBN 1-56308-338-8
        1. Weather--Study and teaching. 2. Meteorology--Study and
teaching. 3. Weather--Bibliography. 4. Meteorology--Bibliography.
5. Interdisciplinary approach in education. I. Title. II. Series.
QC981.5.P47   1995
551.6'071'2--dc20   95-32793
                                                                CIP

For

all the librarians and media specialists
who have enriched my life,
especially my good friend, BJ,
and with special thanks to four remarkable people
at the Boulder Public Library:

Jennifer Fakolt
Mary Jane Holland
Mary McCarthy
Thomas Youtz

Contents

Part I
Snow, Hail, and Ice

Part II
Drought, Dust, and Dunes

Part III
Clouds, Rain, and Floods

Part IV
Winds: Hurricanes, Tornadoes, and Typhoons

Part IV
Winds: Hurricanes, Tornadoes, and Typhoons
(*continued*)

Part V
Additional Resources and Linkages

About the Series

In the era of literature-based reading programs, students are involved in narrative plots more than ever before, but they still face difficulty when confronted with expository text. Many experts believe that one of the best ways to teach anything is to engage the learner, that is, to get the student interested enough in a topic that the motivation to learn increases.

The Literature Bridges to Science series seeks to use the power of fictional works to bring students from the world of imagination into the world of the factual. In this series, fiction is used to build interest, increase familiarity with a topic, enlarge background, and introduce vocabulary. The fiction is to be enjoyed, letting the power of the story create a desire to learn more about a topic. Several fictional works are used, to suit individual tastes and the spread of experience in a group of students.

As student interest builds naturally, one or more "bridge" titles are used to pique interest in a topical exploration. At this point, the teacher may introduce a main theme of study to the class, being confident that the learners are not starting at ground zero in their background knowledge of that topic. Interest in the topic might then be high enough to motivate the learners to engage the expository writing in nonfiction works.

Just as several fictional works are used to introduce a topic, the Literature Bridges to Science series suggests that numerous nonfiction works be offered to students as they begin their topical explorations. Thus, the series is particularly useful to those teachers who are transforming their teaching style to a cross-curricular approach. Nonfiction titles collected here represent the more literary treatments of a topic, in contrast to a textbook-like stream of facts.

Introduction

This book is designed to assist busy teachers planning a middle-grade integrated unit of study involving regions of the world and weather. It includes suggestions for individual, small-group, and large-group activities across the disciplines. The multiple titles allow for student choice based on interest and skill level. The titles were selected from a large number of books recommended by children's librarians with special expertise in books for young adults.

Between the fiction and nonfiction books listed in each section are books that are suggested to serve as "bridges." These bridges are books that enable the reader to make an easy transition from one type of reading material to another. Sometimes they are biographies; sometimes they contain diary or journal entries; and other times they are based on newspaper accounts of a major weather disaster, contain science experiments that will clarify aspects of weather forecasting, or draw attention to environmental problems of the world.

In parts I, II, III, and IV are detailed summaries of fiction books with discussion starters for each book, summaries of related nonfiction books of various lengths and levels of difficulty, and ideas for multidisciplinary activities arising out of both types of books. All suggested books have been published after 1980 and are readily available. The activities involve skills in research, oral and written language, science, mathematics, geography, and the arts.

Each part begins with a "bookweb" suggesting a variety of ideas for discussions and projects that might come out of a study of the fiction, nonfiction, and bridging materials.

📖 Teaching Methods 📖

One Teacher with Multiple Teaching Responsibilities

This book is designed to be used in a variety of different teaching situations. In some cases, a single teacher will be responsible for teaching a variety of subjects to a group of students. If the same teacher is responsible for teaching language arts, social studies, and science, the multidisciplinary approach suggested in this book will have a unifying effect on the curriculum.

Before beginning this unit on the world's regions and weather, the teacher might choose, for example, one of the fiction books and present it as a read-aloud in class. This will help set the tone for the unit of study to come. As students hear a good piece of fiction, such as *Frozen Fire*, they will learn vocabulary and begin to focus on ice, cold, Arctic exploration, survival, and the mineral wealth of frozen lands.

The teacher might suggest that students be alert to information about weather and regions of the world. Encourage students to bring to class articles that they clip from newspapers and magazines, which could be used to create a classroom vertical file. Alert the class (or have students alert their classmates) to opportunities for viewing television specials that focus on weather or some region of the world. Videocassette copies of many of these television specials are available for purchase and would make good additions to the school media center.

When this unit of study begins, the teacher might have each student select one of the fiction titles in part I, and then encourage small-group discussions and sharing among those who have read the same book. This will extend reading skills, listening skills, and the use of oral language.

The teacher might want to work with the class when using a bridge book, to assist students who do not feel as comfortable in reading nonfiction as they do in reading fiction. Edmund Hillary and Susan Butcher, who are featured in the bridge books of part I, should have strong appeal for students because of their real-life adventures. Students might already be familiar with these celebrities. These bridge books may pique student interest in reading about other explorers or other famous sled racers and their dog teams. Students' growing vocabulary and knowledge about snowy regions, hail, and ice will be assets in learning to appreciate nonfiction.

As a composition activity, the teacher might assign writing topics that deal with weather or some region of the world. This might be combined with a science assignment. A student studying the conditions that brought about the Dust Bowl, for example, will need to do library research, learn appropriate procedures for footnoting and preparing a bibliography, and write a cause-and-effect essay.

As a creative writing activity, have students, for example, write original "incidents" (not included in the fiction book currently under discussion) that might have taken place, using the characters and setting in the fiction book. Or, introduce poetry that is related to seasons of the year or weather. Have students read poems and then experiment with writing their own.

Depending upon the books selected for this unit, the teacher might combine history and geography in an activity where students trace the migration to California of many of the original Dust Bowl residents and the social problems that they faced. The focus might be expeditions to the North Pole, or the camel caravans that cross the desert regions.

Departmentalization with Team Planning

In schools where there is departmentalization with team planning time, the language arts, social studies, mathematics, and science teachers might plan a segment of time for a unit on the world's regions and weather.

The language arts teacher might assign reading, research, and writing assignments based on the fiction and nonfiction books. Panel discussions and oral presentations of material will reinforce students' speaking and listening skills. Specific skills such as skimming, reading for information, note taking, outlining, and using an index or a glossary of terms might also be introduced or reinforced using the suggested nonfiction books.

The social studies teacher might discuss Arctic and Antarctic explorations; the Dust Bowl; the gold rush to the Klondike; settlements along sea coasts and rivers; and adaptations in housing, food, clothing, religion, and the arts, depending upon the various climatic regions being studied.

The science teacher might discuss life in temporary spring pools created by melting snow; "singing sands"; the causes and effects of rain and flooding; the depletion of the world's tropical rainforests; weather disasters; and the instruments used in weather forecasting.

The mathematics teacher might discuss various calculations related to the use of weather instruments.

Some students will find it easy to take in information that is presented as pictures or as graphs and charts in the nonfiction books. For other students, these will be new sources of information. Explain how to "read" these special materials, and create assignments that involve students in constructing graphs and charts.

Specialist teachers might also be involved in this unit. The music teacher might incorporate songs and chants from different regions or the world, or might work with the science teacher in explaining such phenomena as "singing sands." The art teacher might explore the different materials used in the artistic expression of people of the various regions of the world, or the symbols used by different groups of Native Americans in depicting weather conditions in their weavings and pottery. Arrange for classroom and hallway bulletin boards to feature topics related to the world's regions and weather.

If the school has a computer lab, introduce students to software that deals with regions of the world, weather forecasting, and weather mapping. Have students use word-processing software for their written reports related to this unit of study.

If the media specialist is responsible for teaching research skills to students, he or she might create activities that focus on topics that can be researched in CD-ROM encyclopedias (e.g., weather), vertical files (e.g., deserts of the world), or computer databases (e.g., hurricanes). The media specialist might highlight magazines and books in the school media center that deal with weather and regions of the world, or might use interlibrary loans to increase the materials available during this unit.

Team Teaching

In schools where team teaching occurs, the various team members might opt to present their favorite lessons and experiments. Choices might be based on personal expertise or interest in a new topic. Next, teachers might map out a sequence and timeline for their students that shows the connections between various subject areas.

While one teacher is presenting a lesson, colleagues might assist by leading small-group discussions, providing assistance for science experiments, or supervising small-group or individual research in the media center.

Some activities in a team teaching situation can be presented to a large group of students, such as films or videos, or inviting an expert to speak about a particular topic. After the large-group presentation, team members might create and lead related break-out groups that give students the opportunity to apply and extend their knowledge.

📖 Culminating Activities 📖

Whatever the configuration of students and teachers, there might well be an opportunity for a special culminating activity for each part of this unit of study. The teacher might present an engaging problem. To solve the problem, students must use what they have learned. In some instances of creative problem solving, local experts might be invited to discuss students' solutions to the problem.

For example, in part II, a question is posed: whether the deserts of the world hold promise or threat for the world's population. Have students research this topic and come up with their own assessment. What are the variables involved? Which of these are controlled by humans? What economic factors are involved? Are there specific actions that must be taken to ensure one result or the other?

As a culminating activity for part III, on the causes and effects of rain, have groups of students construct simple weather instruments and then predict the weather for a period of time. Are student predictions as accurate, less accurate, or more accurate than the weather predictions presented in newspapers and on television? Is one group of students more accurate than other groups in making predictions? Why?

📖 Scope and Sequence 📖

Part I links the regions of snow, hail, and ice. The fiction books include contemporary fiction and fantasy. Each book deals with some aspect of surviving in a cold and frozen world. The nonfiction books are related to climbing high peaks in frozen mountains, racing sled dogs, and learning more about such topics as snow, ice, spring pools, and snowflakes.

Part II links drought, dust, and dunes. The fiction books include survival stories, adventure, and fantasy—an archeological dig, a future space/time travel, and a fantasy set in the barren desert island of Roshan, to name a few. The nonfiction books provide information to help students understand deserts, droughts, and the special part of American history surrounding the Dust Bowl.

Part III links clouds, rain, and floods. The fiction books include contemporary fiction and fantasy. A story of being trapped in a canyon during a flash-flood and surviving the flooding of an entire community when a dam breaks is a contemporary theme. Also included are more gentle tales—of collecting honeysuckle rain and continuing family traditions, for example. The nonfiction books are related to clouds, weather prediction, rains, and storms.

Part IV links winds—hurricanes, tornadoes, and typhoons. The fiction books include contemporary and historical fiction—stories of fierce winds at sea, of a night of twisters in Nebraska, to name two themes. The nonfiction books discuss such topics as storm warnings, weather, and the disastrous effects of hurricanes and tornadoes.

Part V contains additional resources and linkages. Included here are questions that link various fiction books with one another, as well as ideas for using picture books with middle-grade readers. This section concludes with listings of additional fiction and nonfiction books that might be used in the classroom.

Part I
Snow, Hail, and Ice

Snow, Hail, and Ice

● FICTION ●

📖 *Dogsong*
Gary Paulsen

📖 *Frozen Fire*
James Houston

📖 *Ice Warrior*
Ruth Riddell

📖 *Shiva: An Adventure of the Ice Age*
J. H. Brennan

◆ BRIDGES ◆

📖 *The World's Great Explorers: Edmund Hillary*
Timothy R. Gaffney

📖 *Susan Butcher and the Iditarod Trail*
Ellen M. Dolan

■ NONFICTION CONNECTIONS ■

📖 *The Conquest of Everest*
Mike Rosen

📖 *Racing Sled Dogs: An Original North American Sport*
Michael Cooper

📖 *Snow: Causes and Effects*
Philip Steele

📖 *Snow, Ice and Cold: Repairing the Damage*
Bernard Stonehouse

📖 *Snowflakes*
Joan Sugarman

📖 *Spring Pool: A Guide to the Ecology of Temporary Ponds*
Ann Downer

—OTHER TOPICS TO EXPLORE—

—Sledding	—Mountaineering	—Snowshoes	—The Ice Age
—Train snow sheds	—The South Pole	—Caribou	—Winter Olympics
—The North Pole	—Glaciers	—Avalanches	—Polar bears
—Skiing	—Icebergs	—Titanic	—Magnetic North
—Snow making	—Snow plows		

From *The World's Regions and Weather.* © 1996. Teacher Ideas Press. (800) 237-6124.

● *Fiction* ●

📖 *Dogsong*
Gary Paulsen

📖 *Frozen Fire*
James Houston

📖 *Ice Warrior*
Ruth Riddell

📖 *Shiva: An Adventure of the
Ice Age*
J. H. Brennan

 *Dogsong*

FICTION

by Gary Paulsen
New York: Bradbury Press, 1985. 177p.

Type of Book:
This is a survival and adventure book set in the world of ice, snow, and sled dogs, but it is interlaced with a dream, which gives the story a magical quality.

Setting:
The story takes place in a small Eskimo village and to the far north of that village.

Major Characters:
Russel Susskit, 14 years old; his father; Oogruk, a villager who owns dogs and teaches Russel about the old ways; and Nancy, a woman-girl who Russel finds half dead in the snow.

Other Books by the Author:
Dancing Carl (New York: Bradbury Press, 1983); *Hatchet* (New York: Bradbury Press, 1987); and *The Monument* (New York: Delacorte Press, 1991).

—PLOT SUMMARY—

Part one is called "The Trance." The story begins as Russel Susskit awakens in his small, government-owned winter house in a little Eskimo village on the seacoast. Russel hates the sound of his father coughing, which he hears every morning. He also hates his box-like house. The walls are covered with pictures of Jesus. Although Russel does not really understand Jesus, he knows that Jesus somehow keeps his father from drinking, which is good.

The sounds of a passing "snowmachine" annoy Russel, who only uses his own snowmachine to get around because he doesn't have any dogs. All the dogs in his village are owned by old Oogruk.

As Russel cooks some meat for breakfast, he talks with his father about the "old ways" and how things have changed. Finally Russel tells his father that, although he does not know what is wrong, he is not happy with himself. His father has also noticed that something is wrong

but does not think that Russel can find help in Jesus, so he suggests that the boy go to Oogruk for help. Oogruk offers not only words but also may give Russel a song, and a song is always true.

Russel goes to Oogruk's house and stops outside to look at the five dogs near the food cache. He also prepares himself to enter the house, because Oogruk lives in the "old way." He does not use electricity to light his house; he uses a seal-oil lamp. Also, the house is filled with strange smells.

Inside, Russel sits down to listen to Oogruk. He puts on a pan of snow to heat the eyes from two caribou heads that he has brought as a present for the old man. Oogruk offers Russel one of the eyes, but the boy refuses. Oogruk says when Russel is gone "for the long time," he will wish he'd eaten them. Russel asks what the old man means about being gone for the long time, but instead of answering, Oogruk tells him another story. The old man clearly knows what Russel is thinking, including Russel's belief that his village didn't take a whale this year because snowmachines frightened the whales and seals away.

Russel goes out to the food cache and cuts some caribou meat to heat while they talk. Back in the house, he looks at the animal skins, old tools, and weapons hanging on the walls. He comments that similar ones are in the museum in town. But Oogruk is not interested in town, and says they used to have songs in the village until a missionary came and told them they would all go to hell if they didn't stop singing and dancing. So the villagers stopped and the old songs were lost.

Russel decides to try to live the right way again, the old way, and to get a song—to be a song. Oogruk agrees to teach him. In a sort of trance, Russel listens. Much later, he comes out of his trance and prepares to go outside. He takes off his store clothes and dresses in the skins that hang from Oogruk's walls, putting on bearskin pants, sealskin mukluks, a squirrel-skin inner parka, and an outer parka of thick deer hide. He then dons deer-hide mittens and ventures into the cold to harness the dogs to the sled.

At first the lead dog challenges Russel, but using what he learned during his trance, Russel masters the dog. When he has all five dogs in harness, he takes them out for a run to get the feel of the sled and the dogs. At first he is clumsy, but gradually the sled and dogs begin to feel natural to him. They finally return to Oogruk's.

In the days that follow, Russel lives with Oogruk. He goes out in the sled and hunts rabbit and ptarmigan, using the old weapons from the cabin. At first he is clumsy, but gradually he learns how to wield them. Finally he successfully kills both a bird and a deer. He shares meat with the dogs and takes some of the food back to Oogruk. As he goes home from the hunt, part of a "dog song" comes to him.

Later, Russel goes out onto the ice to hunt a seal in the old way. A storm blows up, and Russel hides before it hits. He and the dogs huddle under an overlapping ice ledge with the tipped sled across the opening to block the wind. When the storm ends, Russel heads the dogs for home. They hesitate, but he urges them on. Only later he realizes that the plate of ice he and the dogs had been on was turned around during the storm, and that he ran the dogs in the wrong direction. He then lets the dogs pick the way, and they head for home. However, they discover open water between them and the land ice. Russel bridges the water with a chunk of floating ice, gets back onto the land ice, and safely heads for home.

Russel continues to learn and hunt, but he can get only "light meat." He needs to find caribou or seal to feed the dogs, so one morning he gets up early to hunt seal again. To his astonishment, Oogruk accompanies him. When they reach the ice, Oogruk tells the boy not to go back to the village but to "run long" and find himself. Russel reluctantly leaves the old man, and heads north, but then returns to find Oogruk sitting on the edge of the ice, dead. After Russel performs a ceremony for the old man, he turns his dogs north again.

Part two is called "The Dreamrun." Russel heads out into the north and runs the dogs for 18 hours. After they rest, they set out again and find a herd of caribou. He shoots four with arrows to get food for himself and the dogs. That night, snuggled warm between layers of caribou fur, Russel has a dream in which he clearly sees a woman and two children. Dimly, he also sees a man. The man harnesses strange-looking dogs and goes off to hunt a woolly mammoth. When Russel finally is able to see the man clearly, he recognizes the man as himself. The hunt is successful, and the man sings his special song.

The next day, Russel and his dogs are ready to run again. He is not sure why and where the dogs are running, but they seem to know. After many hours, they stop and camp. When Russel tries to sleep, he finds a lump beneath him. He digs out the lump, which turns out to be a very old oil lamp. He fashions a wick for it and uses caribou fat for oil.

That night, Russel dreams that the man who killed the mammoth goes to a native camp and is warmly greeted by those who live there. The man performs a dance showing how he killed the mammoth. Other men also dance.

The next day, Russel packs his things, and he and the dogs run a long time until they encounter some tracks from a snowmachine. Russel lets the dogs follow the tracks. Later, he has another dream. This time the man in his dreams is fighting to move forward in a terrible storm. The woman and children he left at home are starving.

Russel finally comes upon the abandoned snowmachine, which is cold and out of gas. No one is near it, but small footprints lead away from it. A storm hits, but Russel pushes the dogs forward, following the trail, because anyone left alone out there would perish.

Finally they find a figure in the snow. Russel quickly sets up a camp. When he has the person safely inside a lean-to formed from caribou skins, he lights the oil lamp to discover that he has found a pregnant young woman. As Russel eats, he waits beside the unconscious, half-frozen woman. Then he falls asleep and dreams of the man fighting in the storm. In this dream, the storm finally passes, and the man returns to his home,

to find nothing left but two bones; the woman and children have died of starvation and were eaten by animals. A fox has dragged off the oil lamp. When Russel awakes, he realizes that his oil lamp is also the lamp in his dream, and the face of the pregnant girl is the face of the woman from his dream.

Russel learns that the girl, Nancy, had deliberately gone out in the snowmachine to die because she is not married and has no parents. Her baby is not due for another four months. Because she has no home to go back to, she asks if she can go on the run north with Russel, and he agrees.

They travel for several days and then run out of food. Russel leaves Nancy in a shelter and goes to hunt. After several days without food, Russel hallucinates and starts to despair when he discovers the tracks of a bear. He kills the bear and returns to Nancy with the meat. But she is ill; the baby is coming prematurely and, when it is born, it is stillborn. As Nancy needs medical attention, Russel puts her in the sled along with as much meat as he can carry and begins to run toward a coastal village.

The last, very short portion of the book, part three, is called "Dogsong." In it is the song for which Russel has searched.

📖 Discussion Starters 📖

Dogsong
by Gary Paulsen

1   In Russel's Eskimo village, things are different from what you are accustomed to. Russel does not knock when he enters Oogruk's home. When he moves in with Oogruk, his father approves and thinks this is natural. When Russel does not go to school, no one mentions this because it would not be polite. What other differences do you notice between your customs and ways and those in Russel's world?

2   After Russel has killed his first caribou in the old way and prepared it to take home, his hands get very cold and stiff for a few minutes. He pulls on his mittens, and as his hands warm, he smiles at the cold pain. He thinks of cold "not as an enemy but as many different kinds of friend, or a complicated ally." Why does Russel think of cold as a friend? In what way is cold a complicated ally?

3   One of the lessons that Oogruk teaches Russel is that "It isn't the destination that counts. It is the journey. That is what life is. A journey. Make it the right way and you will fill it correctly with days." Discuss this lesson and what it means to you.

4   Throughout the story, the author uses the expression "folded into." Life and the dream seem to "fold into each other." This happens so many times that Russel can no longer decide what is life and what is a dream. But he believes that being able to distinguish between the two is not important "because the dream was more real than . . . his life." How can a dream be more real than life? Discuss this.

5   Although they are very important, none of the dogs in this story has a name. Why do you suppose the dogs are nameless?

6   Religion plays an unusual role in this story. Russel does not like the religious pictures on the wall and says he cannot understand Jesus, though he does appreciate that in some strange way Jesus keeps his father from drinking. However, Oogluk says it is a missionary who caused the people of the village to stop singing and dancing and to lose their songs. Also, Nancy runs away to die because the missionaries told her that it was a sin to be unmarried and pregnant. Discuss the way religion is treated in this story.

7   Killing an animal in this story involves ceremony. Go back over the various kills that Russel makes. What does he say and do each time? Is the ceremony around the killing significant?

8   When Oogluk orders Russel to go and leave him on the ice to die, Russel goes. Later he comes back, but Oogluk is already dead. If you were in Russel's position, would you have left Oogluk, or would you have stayed or tried to get him medical help?

9   Each of the chapters in part one begins with a short excerpt in italics that is represented as something told by an old Eskimo. Part two does not contain any of these Eskimo sayings. Why do you think they are in part one and not in part two? What is their purpose?

10 Discuss the Dogsong. In one way, it seems to be a footnote added to the end of the story. In another way, it can be seen as the whole purpose of the story. What do you see as the role of the Dogsong?

📖 Multidisciplinary Activities 📖

Dogsong
by Gary Paulsen

1 Although the reader is finally rewarded with the Dogsong in the last section of the book, there is no music. What sort of musical accompaniment or chanting rhythm seems appropriate? Compose music for the Dogsong and record it by playing, singing, or chanting. You might want to try several versions before you have one that sounds right to you. When you are satisfied, share it with the class.

2 The reader is never given the name of the Eskimo village in which Russel lives. Nor are we given the names of any of the places to which he travels north. Find a detailed map of the coastline from Greenland and Labrador in the east to the Bering Sea in the west and the Siberian shore near the Bering Strait. Using what you know from the descriptions given in the story, map out a possible place for Russel's village and the route he took in finding Nancy and returning to the coastline. Share your map with the class.

3 Many different kinds of dogs have successfully been used as sled dogs. Do some research into sled dogs that are famous for their racing feats or heroic deeds. Try to find pictures of these dogs and to identify the different breeds. Choose one dog that you admire. Draw the dog using any medium you prefer (charcoal, pen and ink, pastels, oils, colored pencil, etc.). Share your finished picture with your classmates and tell them a little about the history of this dog.

 *Frozen Fire*

by James Houston
New York: Atheneum, 1983. 149p.

Type of Book:
This is a contemporary adventure survival story and is based in part on a true story. It is told in the third person from the viewpoint of Matthew Morgan.

Setting:
Near Frobisher Bay in the Canadian Arctic.

Major Characters:
Matthew Morgan, 13 years old; his father; Matt's Eskimo friend, Kayak; and Mr. Morgan's friend Charlie, a helicopter pilot.

Other Books by the Author:
Songs of the Dream People (New York: Atheneum, 1972); *Drifting Snow: An Arctic Search* (New York: Macmillan, 1992); and *Wolf Run* (New York: Harcourt Brace Jovanovich, 1971).

—PLOT SUMMARY—

The story begins early in the morning in an airport in Montreal. Matt Morgan and his father, a geologist, are about to fly to Baffin Island, 2,000 miles north into the Canadian Arctic, to look for copper deposits. Matthew has moved so many times in his life that one more move doesn't surprise him much. They climb aboard a tiny plane that carries 12 passengers. Among the passengers is an Eskimo man on crutches who is being attended by a nurse. Matt wishes his mother were with them, but she is dead, and his father rather gruffly reminds him that "wishing won't change anything." Mr. Morgan is certain that they will find their fortune in this new land.

The plane almost crashes in the Arctic wind, but it lands safely. When Matt and his father get out, they find that most of the people in the airport are Eskimos. They are met by Charlie, an Australian helicopter pilot and a friend of Matt's dad. Charlie points to a hangar where he keeps his helicopter, *Waltzing Matilda*.

The Eskimo on crutches is met by his family. While the nurse phones for an ambulance, the man beckons to Matt and says that his son, Kayak, has learned to speak English in school. Kayak asks Matt to tell the nurse that he has driven his father home in a snowmobile. Matt gives the nurse the message and then leaves in a truck with his father and Charlie. They go to a government house that has been loaned to them.

While Matt carries in their belongings, his face gets frostbitten. As his face gradually warms, they check out the kitchen, where there are a few supplies. Charlie promises to come tomorrow and bring them a special fish. After Charlie leaves, Matt and his father have a simple meal. The next morning, Matt goes out in the cold to get some ice to melt on the stove.

Matt enrolls in a school that looks a lot like a spaceship. Among the students in eighth grade is Kayak. When the teacher isn't looking, Kayak uses a file to make a *nanungwak*, or polar bear luck charm, from a bear's tooth.

It is dark when the boys walk home from school together at four o'clock. Kayak tells Matt that in a town 150 miles away lives a girl who has been promised to him as a wife. Matt is amazed that Kayak is even thinking about marriage. Inside Matt's house, his father and Charlie study maps. They plan to fly in search of copper in a few days unless a storm that has been forecast moves in and delays them.

The next day after school, Kayak invites Matt to his house in Apex. Two of Kayak's cousins, Namoni and Ashoona, give them a ride there on a snowmobile. These Eskimos speak Inuktitut. They call Matt "Mattoosie." In Kayak's house, Matt sees the boy's father, Tugak, and also meets Kayak's mother and grandmother. Matt is impressed by a carving that Tugak made of a polar bear. It was carved from a piece of whale bone that Tugak found on the beach.

Matt returns home to find his father getting ready to leave the next morning. His father is looking at a piece of native copper that an Eskimo had brought into Frobisher the previous October. His father does not think the piece of native copper came from the place where the Eskimo found it, but from a different area. He believes that it was dragged from the mother lode by a glacier. By studying a map, Mr. Morgan helps Matt understand where the copper might really be. Charlie has not been told about this because he talks too much at night when he is celebrating with his friends. Mr. Morgan wants to start searching right away, because he believes other geologists will study the new topographic maps and beat him to a claim on the copper.

When Charlie arrives, he brings news that some miners are flying in with a lot of equipment, but they may be delayed because a storm is brewing. Mr. Morgan insists on flying out in the morning, and he deliberately gives the wrong destination to Charlie so that the filed flight plan will not reveal the secret of where they have really gone.

The next day, a big storm blows in, and Matt hopes his father and Charlie have turned around and flown home again. But when he gets home from school, no one is there, and the power has gone out. Matt lights a candle and the propane stove. Two Mounties come by to check on him and try to reassure him that his father and Charlie will fly back tomorrow.

School is closed the next day because of the wind. Kayak comes to visit and brings fish to eat. That afternoon the two boys go over to the radio shack to see if anyone has heard anything from Mr. Morgan and Charlie. The radio operator tells Matt that they have heard nothing from the missing men. At midnight they will turn the matter over to Air Force Search and Rescue, which is located in Greenwood, Nova Scotia.

The Royal Canadian Mounted Police (RCMP) and the Air Force Search and Rescue arrive the next day. Matt tries to tell them that the flight plan is incorrect, but they don't listen. The RCMP pilot says they will search at six in the morning and invites Matt, Kayak, and the radio operator to come with him.

The next day, two planes take off on an unsuccessful search. They are joined the next day by a third plane. At the end of the search, Matt finds a chance to suggest where he thinks his father and Charlie really flew. On their way back, they fly over this new area, and Kayak thinks he spots the red helicopter.

The next day, fog keeps the planes from going up. Matt realizes they may not be able to fly again for a week. Using his father's maps, he works out their position, which is 96 miles away. Kayak suggests that they borrow his cousin's snowmobile and go out looking for the two men if the planes are grounded again. This turns out to be the case, so Kayak and Matt set off. They travel for hours, rest, and continue the next day. The going is treacherous, but things are going well until they discover that the gas can has leaked and that they are almost out of fuel. They decide to try to find the helicopter, hoping it will still have gasoline. When the snowmobile finally stops, Matt removes the mirror and takes it with him. They walk as far as they can and then put up their tent against the wind.

The next day is clear, and they walk again. At night, Kayak shoots a rabbit that they eat after digging a hole and making a shelter. The next day there is a whiteout and they cannot search. Kayak says they must try to go back to the village, but Matt doesn't want to leave without having found his father. Still, they set out, only to wander in a circle and end up back at their shelter.

The next day they head for home again, this time placing markers as they go along. Over the past few days, a wolf has been howling and coming closer to them. Today they actually see it, but it slinks away. Then Kayak falls into an icy canyon. Using a rope, Matt rescues his friend, but their tent is torn and they lose the rifle, their knife, and Kayak's dark glasses.

They walk onward and suddenly see strange beings. They find and enter a dwelling where there are a man, a woman, and some children. Curved rib bones of a whale support the roof of the dwelling. The house has a bed and lots of furs, blankets, and clothing. The wife gives them food, and the husband explains that he once lived in Frobisher but moved away when it became crowded. The next day the man sends them on their way again with three presents: a plastic bow with arrows, a snow knife, and caribou meat. He also gives them directions to return home. He tells them not to come back looking for him, because he and has family will have moved by then. The wife gives them charms to wear and provides Kayak with a pair of homemade dark glasses.

As Matt and Kayak travel, they stop at a calm spot below a rushing waterfall, and Matt pulls a yellow pebble from the water. Then an owl lands near them, and Matt tries to shoot it. The bow breaks in the cold. Kayak tells Matt it would have been bad luck to kill the owl. Matt goes to the spot where the owl was perched. He thinks he sees frozen fire there, and when he looks more closely, he sees many gold nuggets in the area. Kayak is unimpressed and takes only a small flintstone, but Matt picks up many gold nuggets.

The next day Matt struggles along with a heavy pack of gold, but he eventually abandons it.

The boys finally get close enough to see the lights of Frobisher, but the ice has cracked and they are cut off. Kayak tries to float them across the water gap on a chunk of ice, but they cannot get to land. As they float toward the sea, an immense polar bear climbs up onto the ice pan and moves toward them. The boys stay still, and the bear continues to a spot where it kills and eat a seal before slipping back into the water.

Matt and Kayak form a shelter of ice and pull the remains of the seal into the shelter. Then, using his flintstone and a bit of steel wool, Kayak manages to make a fire by using a wick in the seal fat stuffed into the seal's heart. Warmed by the fire, the boys eat strips of the seal. They run about to get warmer and then sleep through the night.

In the morning they see a plane overhead. Using the mirror from the snowmobile, Matt tries to signal them. The plane does not turn around, so Matt is uncertain whether or not his signal has been seen.

Then the ice breaks up again, and the boys lose their sleeping bags and pack. That night, Kayak makes a circle of seal blood around their shelter. Believing they will soon die, they huddle by their lamp and eat some seal meat.

Alerted by the report that a signal had been spotted by a Nordair pilot, Charlie arrives to search the area by helicopter. Attracted by the red circle around the shelter, Charlie arrives in a helicopter and drops a ladder to the boys. His leg is injured, but he is otherwise all right. He brings the boys back to the village and to a hospital. The boys learn that Matt's father had hiked out for help from the helicopter crash and is suffering from frostbite and exhaustion.

Matt and his father are reunited in the hospital. For the time being, Matt keeps his secret about the gold nuggets, and Matt's father tells the happy boys that he has found a teaching job, so they will be staying on Baffin Island.

📖 Discussion Starters 📖

Frozen Fire
by James Houston

1   Kayak is not very interested in what is being taught at his school. He wants to learn about hunting and carving. Is Kayak realistic? What would schooling have to offer him?

2   At age 13, Matt has already lived in many different places and attended several schools. When he goes to the Arctic, he says he leaves no friends behind him because he hasn't been there long enough to make friends. If you were forced to move often, how might you feel about school? Do you think it would become easier or more difficult to adjust to a new place each time you moved?

3   What did you think of the "wild man" and his family? This man says he doesn't want to live somewhere where his children will be taught to be different from him. He wants to bring them up wild and free. Do you think the "wild man" has chosen a good life? Why or why not?

4   The "wild man" wears several wristwatches, but he has torn the hands off all of them. Does this make any sense? Why is this detail included in the story?

5   The image of a polar bear is found throughout the story. Look back through the book and find the places where a polar bear is mentioned. Is this recurring theme effective? What is its role in the story?

6   Matt throws away the gold nuggets, but Kayak keeps a small piece of flint that saves their lives. When Kayak first mentions that the flint is more valuable than gold, did you have an inkling that the flint would be used later to save them? If you had been Matt, would you have thrown away all the gold?

7   Matt and Kayak become good friends very quickly in the story. Why do you think this happens so fast?

8   The title of the book, *Frozen Fire*, comes from the scene when Matt discovers the gold nuggets. If you were naming this book, what title would you give it and why?

9   When the story ends, Mr. Morgan is planning to live a more settled life and to be a teacher. Do you think he will stick with this when he is well, or will he go off seeking minerals again?

10 Matt doesn't tell his father about the gold nuggets when he is reunited with him in the hospital. How long do you think it will be before Matt tells him, or will he keep the gold a secret forever? If Matt does tell his father about the gold, how do you think his father will react?

📖 **Multidisciplinary Activities** 📖

Frozen Fire
by James Houston

1   As soon as the book opens, the reader is presented with many geographic names that are used to help create its setting. Many of these are small Eskimo villages. Using a detailed map of the area, try to locate the following places that are mentioned in the book: Montreal; Frobisher Bay; the Hudson Straits; Ungava Bay; Moose Jaw, Saskatchewan; the Grinnel Glacier; Baffin Island; Kingmerok; Pangnirtung; Greenwood, Nova Scotia; Cape Dorset; Igloolik; Lake Harbor; and Arctic Bay. Share the map with the marked locations on it with your class.

2   Matt's father is a geologist. Do you know someone in your town who is a geologist? If so, invite that person to visit your class. The geologist might be able to bring in some mineral specimens and to discuss the various types of work that a geologist does. In setting up this class visit, be sure to clear the time with your teacher and to follow up the visit with a thank-you letter.

3   James Houston, the author, drew the book jacket and the small black-and-white sketches at the end of each chapter. Among these small drawings is a stylized picture of a polar bear on page 47. The polar bear is a recurring symbol used throughout the book. Reread chapter 9 in which a huge polar bear comes very close to Matt and Kayak. Make your own black-and-white line drawing of a scene from this chapter that could be used as an illustration for the book.

 *Ice Warrior*

by Ruth Riddell
New York: Atheneum, 1992. 138p.

FICTION

Type of Book:
This is a modern-day, problem-solving story told in the third person from the viewpoint of Rob Marshall.

Setting:
Welholm Falls, Minnesota.

Major Characters:
Seventh grader Rob Marshall; his dad, Larry Marshall; his mother; his stepfather, Jim Erikson; his stepbrother, Doug; his neighbor, Jennifer Johannsen; his teacher, Ms. Pickering; Coach Enge; and several boys of Rob's age, including Smitty and Brian.

Other Books by the Author:
Haunted Journey (New York: Atheneum, 1988) and *Shadow Witch* (New York: Atheneum, 1989).

—PLOT SUMMARY—

The story begins near the end of Christmas vacation. Rob Marshall rereads a note from his father that tells of Rob's father's plans to fly from California to Minneapolis for a February meeting; he will then drive to Welholm Falls on Saturday morning to see Rob. Rob drops the note and hurries out of his room, grabbing his skates, stick, and helmet to hurry to a hockey game; he is a third-string player for the Polar Bears. Coach Enge gives advice and tries to help, but Rob is not yet comfortable on the team, being the new kid in town; also, his mom divorced his dad in California and moved to Welholm Falls to marry one of the high school coaches.

When Rob goes into the game, he tries to act tough, but he is scared, as he is a newcomer to hockey and not good at it. He misses windsurfing and the California beaches. He plays hard but makes a mistake in the game, sprains his ankle, and causes the Polar Bears to lose to the Eskimos. Afterwards, some team members go out for pizza, but they do not ask Rob to come along.

Rob sees a poster announcing the Winter Festival. He thinks to himself that his dad, if his dad were here, would win everything in the festival. His dad is a natural athlete and is very competitive; his dad's motto is, "Winning isn't everything. It's the *only* thing."

That night as Rob soaks his swollen ankle, he dreams of California and windsurfing on the Sun Warrior. His stepbrother Doug looks in on him, and then his mother comes in to talk. She is worried about him. Rob remembers how he was always supposed to put on a happy face for his mother when she dropped him somewhere to be cared for while she worked as a flight attendant. Thus, he cannot explain to her why he is not happy here. One of his worries is how his dad will react when he comes to visit and finds that Rob sprained his ankle and cannot play hockey.

The next day, Doug goes out iceboating and, when he gets home, tells the family that Mr. Enge has a great boat and is sure to win the race at the Winter Festival this year. Rob's mom and Jim, his stepfather, invite Rob to take a ride with them to see the boat, but he refuses to go.

The coach sends over one of the boys, Smitty, to see how Rob is doing. Smitty offers Rob a ride on his iceboat, the Windy Demon, across the lake, so that Smitty can register to be in the Winter Festival. Rob discovers that iceboating is a lot like windsurfing and wonders how long it would take to learn to maneuver an iceboat.

That night at dinner, Rob asks a lot of questions about iceboats. Jim says he can use the DN, a homemade iceboat stored in the boathouse, if he wants to give it a try. Doug points out that he used this iceboat, the Snow Devil, to take fifth place one year and adds that his dad won the Welholm Falls regatta three years running. Rob asks if he can take the Snow Devil out, but his mother will not let him until his ankle heals.

Rob thinks about skipping school but does not after he realizes he would get into serious trouble. Then his teacher, Ms. Pickering, keeps him after school to talk about his poor work. She tells him that unless she sees a lot of improvement, she'll be calling his parents. Reluctantly, Rob goes to the library to work on his overdue book report, and he finds a book on boating. Jennifer's mother, a librarian, walks Rob home and cautions him about how much time it would take to learn to pilot an iceboat. But Rob is already dreaming of winning the trophy in the Festival.

Rob stays up rewriting his science report, doing the new math assignments, and writing a good book report, which wins approval from Ms. Pickering. After school, Rob pulls Jennifer aside, saying that he needs her help with a secret project. The two pull out the ice boat, even though it is terribly cold, only to find that there are holes in the sail. Jennifer runs home for some iron-on patches, and after they apply them, they go out on the ice. Their first try is disastrous; Rob hurts his ankle again. After the second try, Jennifer gets out of the iceboat and heads for home. Rob comes close to crashing into other boys

and their boats, but luckily does no damage to anyone. Brian says Rob's boat is a piece of junk, but Smitty sticks up for Rob.

Rob now takes a good look at the Snow Devil and realizes that it does need repairs. His stepfather, Jim, comes out to the boat house and offers to help make some of the repairs. Rob accepts the offer and, the next day, gets some supplies needed to repair the boat from Mr. Enge, who suggests that Rob's stepfather is the one to teach him about racing.

On the way home, Rob meets Brian and another boy who tease him about even thinking he can race. Rob is in his room almost crying when his stepfather comes up to talk with him. Able to communicate with Rob for the first time, Jim explains that Brian hasn't got a mother or father and is an insecure boy who sees Rob as a threat. Afterwards, Rob goes downstairs to see what Jim and his mother have for him. He finds a helmet, insulated boots and coveralls, a set of ice creepers, and a hand-knitted face mask—all things that he needs, but he feels uncomfortable accepting them from Jim.

In school the next day, Ms. Pickering praises Rob's report. Brian makes a disparaging remark, and Rob proves that Brian doesn't know as much about iceboats as he pretends to. Brian then trips Rob, but Rob shrugs it off as no big deal. Outside of class, Rob apologizes to Jennifer for their disaster on the ice and explains that he feels sorry for Brian.

That night after dinner, Jim, Doug, and Rob begin to repair the Snow Devil. Doug and Jim tell Rob that this boat will be his and that he should give it a new name. Almost speechless with joy, Rob enjoys working with his stepfather and stepbrother. The next day, Rob names his boat the Ice Warrior. Jim approves.

Ms. Pickering reminds the class that they have an art assignment in conjunction with the Winter Festival. Rob can hardly wait for the weekend to come so that he can take the boat out on the ice.

The next day after school, Rob's mother drives Rob and Jennifer to pick up the new sail. The store is out of cloth and so is the store in a town 15 miles away. Because of a strike, no one knows when cloth might be available. Rob worries that all the work on the boat was wasted because he cannot use the boat without a sail. Jim has a friend in Demmering who will try to find cloth for the sail. In the meantime, they have to use the sail with the iron-on patches. Rob tells his mother how good he feels about working with tools and fixing the boat.

Rob goes out to look for shell ice, ice that's frozen on top but has water or air beneath it. Brian challenges Rob to a race right then. Smitty suggests that they go to another spot and practice iceboating while they wait for Jim to join them after a trip to the dentist. Rob becomes intoxicated by the speed of the boat but comes through all right. Jim and Jennifer arrive, bringing a picnic lunch. The iceboaters continue practicing, and that night Jim explains more rules and maneuvers to Rob.

Rob tries to keep up with school work but hasn't yet come up with an idea for the art project, which is due soon. When he takes the Ice Warrior to be inspected so that he can enter the race, the inspector suggests that the position of the runner plank might slow him down. Rob picks up a bundle of festival posters to distribute. When Rob goes back outside, he finds two boys from his class, Brian and Charlie, climbing all over his boat. Rob and Brian fight, and Rob gives Brian a bloody nose, though he himself is shaky after this, his first fist fight.

Monday, Brian looks fine but Rob sports a bruise from the fight. Ms. Pickering reminds Rob that his art project is due tomorrow. When Rob gets home, he comes up with an idea using the posters. He cuts out the hockey players, paints their back sides, and threads green yarn through them. Then he hangs them near red lights in a maple tree in front of the park's office. The next day, Rob tells Ms. Pickering about his project; she says she'll look at it on her way home from school.

Besides everything else, Rob is excited because his dad will be coming tomorrow. The snowy weather is letting up, and conditions should be great for the Winter Festival. The race doesn't begin until two in the afternoon, but Rob gets up early, expecting his dad to appear at any minute. The morning passes, but Rob's father doesn't come. Rob's mother reminds him that he must have total concentration this afternoon to do his best, but that he doesn't have to win or prove himself. She assures Rob that he's a courageous boy. Then, Rob's father calls from the airport in Minneapolis to say that he has another important business meeting in Detroit and can't stop to see Rob on this trip.

Rob's family and friends gather around him just before the race. Jennifer gives him a rabbit's foot for luck. Ms. Pickering says that even through the paint on his cutouts ran, they ended up looking like multicolored icicles. She says she's betting on Rob to win the race.

Rob begins in the middle of the pack, but slowly gains on the others in the race. The position of the runner plank is giving him the stability that he needs to use the sail when winds hit. Then Brian's boat tips over. Instead of going ahead and winning, Rob stops to help Brian.

At the awards ceremony, Rob sees the trophies and ribbons go to others. But he does win first place in the art contest, and Ms. Pickering, Jennifer, Jim, and his mother are all proud of him. The story ends with Brian, Smitty and the other boys asking if Rob wants to go with them to get a pizza.

📖 Discussion Starters 📖

Ice Warrior
by Ruth Riddell

1 The following statement faces page 1 of the book: "Success should not be based on how much one achieves. Rather, it should be based on the number of obstacles one overcomes to achieve." Discuss this.

2 Rob says he feels all mixed up, like scrambled eggs. Yet he wants things to return to what they once were, because even when his parents were fighting, it was better than "being a scrambled nothing, a piece of seaweed, that no one liked." Do you think Rob is being realistic at this point? Were things better before?

3 When he is kept after school, Rob almost discusses some of his problems with Ms. Pickering but decides against it. He thinks to himself that the only things teachers care about are making sure kids can see the blackboard and hear the assignments. Do you agree or disagree with Rob's assessment of teachers?

4 When Rob gets his helmet, mask, coveralls, boots, and face mask, he feels uncomfortable. He goes to his room and arranges them on the bed so that they look like a real person. Then he puts a picture of his father inside the face mask, to make "his dad the iceboat pilot!" Why do you think Rob does this?

5 After Brian trips Rob in class, Rob has an opportunity to blame Brian or to shrug it off. Rob chooses the latter because he feels sorry for Brian. If you were in Rob's position, trying to deal with Brian's hatred for you, what might you do?

6 After they repair the Snow Devil, Rob chooses a new name for his boat. If you were going to name an iceboat, what name would you choose and why?

7 Throughout the book, Rob wrestles with two questions: Must a son believe what his father believes? And does a son have to grow up to be the same kind of man as his father? What do you think?

8 Rob often repeats one of his Dad's favorite expression, "Excuses are for losers." What do you think of this expression?

9 The art contest is mentioned many times in the story. Did you guess well ahead of time that Rob would be the winner, or were you surprised when he won?

10 Rob could have won the race, but he chose to stop and help Brian instead. Were you expecting Rob to win the race, or did you think that something would prevent him from winning?

📖 Multidisciplinary Activities 📖

Ice Warrior
by Ruth Riddell

1 Rob counts on the fact that much of what he knows about windsurfing will transfer over to iceboating. Do some research on both sports. What about them is similar, and what is different? What are the speed records in both sports? In doing your research, interview people who have participated in one or both sports, if possible. Share what you learn about these sports with your classmates.

2 Ms. Pickering points out that it is one thing to know some facts and quite another to understand why and how something takes place. She says: "There are two kinds of knowledge: one that is learned from doing a thing, and the academic kind." Rob says that in his report he explained about the parallelogram of forces, which is the phenomenon of a boat being able to sail into the wind, and he challenges Brian to explain this. Using drawings or diagrams, can you explain the parallelogram of forces to your class and help them understand why a boat can sail into the wind?

3 Throughout the story, the teacher encourages her students to be creative and to submit to her an art project that would depict the spirit of the Winter Festival. Rob decorated a tree with cutouts that accidentally turned into multicolored icicles when the paint ran. Jennifer made a diorama. Do an original piece of art in any media and try to capture the spirit of the Winter Festival. Share your art work with your class.

Shiva: An Adventure of the Ice Age

by J. H. Brennan
New York: J. B Lippincott, 1989. 184p.

Type of Book:
> This book is a fantasy with many flashbacks; it is told in the third person from multiple viewpoints.

Setting:
> Europe, about 30,000 years ago.

Major Characters:
> Shiva, a 12-year-old orphan; Hiram, a young man of Shiva's tribe; the ogre Thag, his wife Hana, and their child Doban; and Renka and the Crone, who are leading women of Shiva's tribe.

Other Books by the Author:
> *Dark Moon* (New York: Holt, Rinehart & Winston, 1980) and the sequel to *Shiva, Shiva Accused: An Adventure of the Ice Age* (New York: HarperCollins, 1991).

—PLOT SUMMARY—

The first two chapters of the book are told from Shiva's point of view. She believes a wolf is following her, and she isn't sure how to reach safety or defend herself. She reflects on misfortunes that have recently struck members of her tribe and hopes that she is not to be the next victim.

The wolf steps out, and Shiva hurls herself at it. Cut and bleeding, she loses her club, so she pulls out her knife. As the wolf approaches again, she sees a strange boy on top of the wolf. The boy bites the wolf and kills it. When certain the wolf is dead, the boy dances around the wolf's body and then comes to Shiva. She tries to talk to him, but he does not speak. Shiva skins the wolf and heads for home; the strange boy follows.

In the next chapter, the viewpoint character is Hiram, a young man of Shiva's tribe, who is very uneasy. Because of an earlier adventure, he does not believe that the Council of the Elder Women will believe what he has to tell them today. While waiting to appear before the Council, Hiram remembers how two summers ago he followed a hippo to a marula grove, where he found many animals feasting on marula fruit. Hiram ate the fruit and experienced strange sensations. He wanted to bring his tribe to the grove, but he was unable to find the spot again. Now, everyone regards Hiram with suspicion.

The fourth chapter is told from the viewpoint of Thag, an ogre, who lives far from Shiva's village. Thag is worried about his missing son, Doban. Thag is also hiding from his wife, Hana. Thag and his men have already unsuccessfully searched everywhere except in the encampment of the Weakling Strangers.

Chapter 5 returns to Hiram's tale. He tries to tell the elders, including the tribe's leader, Renka, and the Crone, about the ogres, whom he saw, but because of the earlier episode with the marula grove, the elders do not believe him.

In the sixth chapter, Shiva returns quietly to her camp with the strange boy (who is Doban). She shows him what to do with the wolf carcass and talks to him while she works. When she is finished, she tells the boy to come with her.

She begins to clean the wolf. When several children come to see what Shiva is doing, the little ogre hides. When the children run off, Doban returns. Then the villagers come and fall upon the little ogre. Shiva is unable to prevent them from taking the boy away.

Chapter 7 switches to Hiram's viewpoint. He waits to hear from the Council and reflects that if they do not believe him, he will never be made keeper of the Sacred Drums. Then a girl runs up to Hiram and tells him that Renka wishes to see him. Expecting to be punished for lying, Hiram instead, learns that he will lead the tribe to battle against the ogres.

Chapter 8 returns the reader to Thag and Hana, who are mourning the death of their son. Hana believes Doban's soul will be reborn in another body. Then Heft, the Hunter, appears and says that Doban is alive and a captive of the Weakling Strangers. Thag and his clan know how the Weakling Strangers came from the south and took all the best game areas and fought the ogres with magic. The ogres remember that time as the Age of Blood. Thag vows to kill the Weakling Strangers and release his son.

Chapter 9 follows Shiva, who remembers a time three years ago when she found the Ring of Stones. She recalls the ancient story of Saber, a wildcat, who thinks he is the largest cat in the world until he meets a lynx. Saber then goes to the Mother of All Things and asks to grow larger than the lynx. The Mother sends Saber to swim in the Pool of Growth but tells him never to go there without her permission and never to drink the water. Saber swims in the pool, grows large, and is content until he meets a spotted leopard who is larger. The Mother sends him to swim in the Pool of Growth again, but afterwards he meets a cave lion who is even larger.

The lion tells Saber that he is a favorite of the Mother, who has promised that other cats will not be allowed to grow as big as he is. So Saber decides to swim in the pool without permission. He grows very large and believes himself to be chief among all creatures, until he meets an enormous woolly mammoth and goes back to the Mother. Noticing that he has already made a trip to the Pool of Growth without her permission, she tells Saber that he can grow no larger and must not return to the Pool of Growth. Saber pretends to obey, but that night goes to the Pool and drinks. He falls asleep, and when he wakes he is a saber-toothed tiger.

Saber tries to attack the Mother for causing him to become the tiger. She throws a stone at him, which falls to Earth; it is now known as a holy place, and the Crone ordered that a ring of stones be placed around it.

Shiva remembers how she came upon the stone, felt dizzy, and touched it. The Crone asked how she had found the ring of stones. Shiva said she had come upon them by accident, but the Crone does not believe this. She says, "nothing—nothing of importance—ever happens by accident." When thinking about the trapped little ogre, Shiva knows that the boy saved her life and reflects that the occurrence was no accident.

As chapter 10 begins, Shiva goes out into the night. The Crone is in a cave crumbling magical herbs with which she makes a fire. In a special bowl of blue water, the Crone sees visions of Hiram, sleeping and afraid of going to war; of the women and the children sleeping; and of Shiva's absence. The Crone also sees Renka feeling fretful.

Meanwhile, Shiva has safely avoided all the guards and made her way to Doban's cage. She frees him and tells him to run away before anyone comes or finds out that Shiva set him free. But the Crone has seen what's happening and alerts the village.

Chapter 11 is Hiram's nightmare. He dreams of being in the forest and getting caught by a monster. When he wakens, he thinks he can still smell the ogres, and asks one of the guards to sniff the air. She reminds him that the reason they smell ogre is because of the one they have caged in the camp.

Hiram retreats to his shelter, then realizes that although the little ogre is to the south, the scent Hiram notices is from the west. Taking an axehead, he goes out to investigate. Suddenly a monstrous shape looms in front of him.

In chapter 12, Shiva still tries to make the little ogre leave, finally turning and running with him. They cross the river, and that night they sleep in the safety of a high tree. When Shiva awakens, the little ogre is gone, but he quickly reappears with food. Shiva thinks of building a shelter, then considers living in a cave. Then a rhino charges.

Chapter 13 focuses on Hana, who is talking to old Hagar and wondering whether or not Thag will rescue Doban and punish the Weakling Strangers. Thag returns and calls out the clan to talk to them. He gives a speech about the search for Doban and brings forward Hiram, their prisoner.

In chapter 14, Renka and her tribe prepare for war. While Renka wonders if it is right to do this, the drums begin beating, and the Crone comes out and does a strange dance. Then the Crone leads the Council into a cave and begins to paint a magic picture. Saber the cat emerges in the drawings. When the Crone is done, Renka leads the warriors to battle.

Chapter 15 returns to the rhino charging Shiva. Shiva tries to outrun it, jumps over a rock, and falls into a cavern. The rhino cannot reach her and leaves. Shiva begins to explore the cavern and comes upon the skull and bones of a sabre-toothed tiger. As she looks into the skull, images begin to form in her mind, as if she were looking into the mists of

the ice age. She thinks if she takes the skull of Saber back to her tribe, they will forgive her for freeing the ogre boy and let her back into the tribe. Leaving the cavern, she looks around for the little ogre but does not see him.

In chapter 16, Hiram goes on trial before the ogres. Hana asks how Thag knows Hiram is the one who stole their son. Thag becomes furious, and in the uproar he creates, Hiram manages to escape. He runs from the cavern and out into the open, where he meets Renka and the others from his tribe.

Shiva tries to find her way through the unfamiliar forest in chapter 17. She brings the skull of Saber with her because she feels she is bound to it in a special way. Then she thinks she is being followed, so she climbs a tree to wait. As she climbs down, she is caught by a large ogre and sees Doban there also. The little ogre tries to speak to her. Finally she realizes he is trying to say in her language, "Shiva, this is Heft, the Hunter."

In chapter 18, Heft carries Shiva back to his clan, with Doban running alongside them. They arrive just in time to see the human tribe meet the ogre clan outside the cave from which Hiram has just escaped. Thag roars a challenge. One of Renka's tribe slings a rock at Thag. Hana steps in front of it and is hit in the head. She falls. Before other blows are struck, Shiva leaps out holding the skull of Saber. Shiva's tribe begins to retreat. Thag is ready to attack, believing they have killed Hana, but she awakens and holds him back. Thag and Hana see Doban holding Shiva's hand. A brief epilogue concludes the book.

📖 Discussion Starters 📖

Shiva: An Adventure of the Ice Age
by J. H. Brennan

1   Frequently in the story, the reader is told that "nothing—nothing of importance—ever happens by accident." Discuss this statement. From your life experience, does it seem to be true?

2   Although she is 12, Shiva talks more to the strange boy who saves her from the wolf than she has ever talked with any boy of the village. Why do you think that Shiva never talks to the boys of her tribe?

3   In Shiva's tribe, the women are the Elders of the Council. In Thag's tribe, women are not supposed to be involved in leadership decisions, but Thag's wife, Hana, always takes an active role in such decisions anyway. What is the effect on the story of having two groups, one ruled by women and one by men?

4   The Crone is a strange figure. Sometimes she is a frail old woman, and at other times she seems possessed by demons and gods. Look at her portions of the story. What would you say her major role was in this book?

5   Thag's clan has a language and Shiva's tribe has a language, but they cannot speak to each other. Only little Doban manages to speak in both tongues. Why is it that the youngest person in the book is the one who tries to speak in both languages?

6   Saber is used as a symbol throughout. His story is told in detail. The Crone paints his picture on the wall. Shiva finds his skull in the cavern. What do you think Saber represents?

7   In many ways, Thag and Hana come across as the most human of the characters. They fight with, support, argue with, and influence each other. Review the Thag and Hana sections. What do they say and do that makes them seem like a modern husband and wife?

8   Does the character of Hiram seem consistent to you? Sometimes he sees or finds things that others don't. He is chosen to lead his tribe to war, yet at the end of the book he rather foolishly falls at Renka's feet and adds nothing to the final scene. Would you expect him to appear in a sequel to the book?

9   What do you think happens after the story? Do the Weakling Strangers go home and leave the ogres alone, or do they battle one another? Do they begin to communicate? Does Shiva return to her tribe or stay with the ogre clan? What are your reasons for thinking as you do?

10   Do you think the epilogue was of value? Did it interest you to know that the story represented the imaginary happenings between Neanderthals and Cro-Magnon people? Would you have chosen to include or exclude the epilogue from the book?

📖 Multidisciplinary Activities 📖

Shiva: An Adventure of the Ice Age
by J. H. Brennan

1 The legend of Saber is similar to many other folktales and legends where a creature is discontented and asks a powerful figure to change it. The legend is also similar because the weaker figure disobeys the powerful figure and does exactly what he has been ordered not to do. Look up some other legends and folktales until you find one that you think is especially similar to the legend of Saber. Share your legend or folktale with your class and point out its similarities and differences.

2 The epilogue states that the events in this story could have taken place because Neanderthals and Cro-Magnon people existed at the same time. Do some research on this topic. Find out when and in what parts of the world Neanderthals and Cro-Magnon people lived. When and where were the major archaeological finds made? What do we know about these early beings and how they lived? Report to the class what you learn. Be sure to cite the sources of information that you used.

3 Shiva has a vision of great sheets of ice and remembers the ballads she has heard of Mamar, God of Ice, and his barren kingdom. What was the Ice Age? When did it occur? What caused it? What were the results of the Ice Age? Could another Ice Age occur? Why or why not? Use a map of the world to show your classmates where the great ice sheets once were. In an oral report, share what you have learned.

♦ *Bridges* ♦

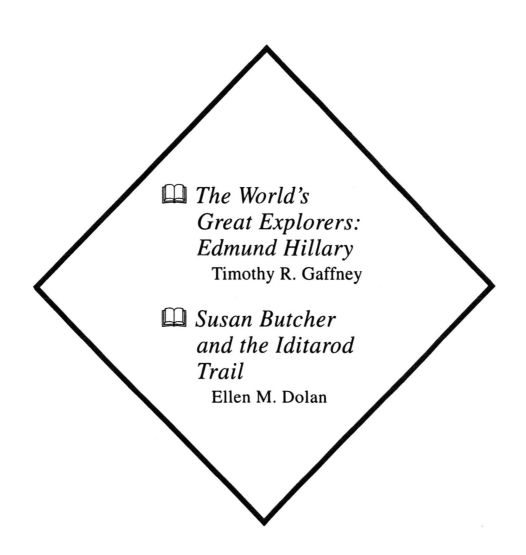

📖 *The World's Great Explorers: Edmund Hillary*
Timothy R. Gaffney

📖 *Susan Butcher and the Iditarod Trail*
Ellen M. Dolan

The World's Great Explorers: Edmund Hillary

BRIDGES

by Timothy R. Gaffney
Chicago: Childrens Press, 1990. 128p.

This is one of a series of books on great explorers. It is illustrated with both color and black-and-white photographs.

Chapter 1 begins with Hillary's climb of Mount Everest, 29,028 feet high, in 1953. He and Tenzing Norgay became the first people to reach the highest point on Earth. The book then traces Hillary's life, starting with his birth in 1919 in Auckland, New Zealand. Hillary grew up on a farm and did not see snow until 1935 when, at age 16, he went with school friends on a ski trip to Mount Ruapehu. In 1940 Hillary went to the Southern Alps on New Zealand's South Island and hired a mountain guide. During World War II, he trained as a navigator and was sent to the South Pacific. After the war, Hillary returned to beekeeping. He made a friend of the well-known New Zealand mountain guide Harry Ayes and began serious climbing in New Zealand, Austria, and Switzerland.

In 1951, Hillary went with the first New Zealand expedition to the Himalayas. Then he was invited to join English explorer Eric Shipton to scout a new route up Mount Everest. Hillary joined the Alpine Club's John Hunt Expedition and was named to the second team that would try to make the summit. When the first team failed, Hillary and Norgay became the first to reach the top. The Queen of England knighted him for his efforts. Other of Hillary's climbs are discussed, including an expedition to Antarctica.

Possible Topics for Further Investigation

1. The portion of the book dealing with Hillary's Antarctic expedition talks about the "true South Pole," the point where the Earth's lines of longitude meet. It is explained that magnetic compasses lose their accuracy that close to the pole. Most people have learned to rely on compass readings, so it is disturbing to think that they are not always accurate. Study this problem. Find out what an astrocompass is and how it is used. Report what you learn to your class.

2. Almost everyone has heard stories about the Abominable Snowman. This book tells that Himalayan Sherpas believed in an apelike animal living in the Himalayas, which they called "yeti." Field Enterprises sponsored an expedition with Hillary to search for yeti in 1960. No one in the group ever saw a yeti. Write an original short story set in the Himalayas. Have your expedition members follow the tracks of a yeti—and find one! Share your story with the class.

3. The joke goes that one of the problems in climbing Mount Everest is to find it! Indeed, it does appear to be in the middle of nowhere. On a map, locate Mount Everest. Identify the countries surrounding it and a few of their important cities. Then try to identify some of the major places mentioned in this book: Makalu, Katmandu, Mingbo Valley, Khumjung, Khunde, the Solu-Khumbu region, Taweche, Kangtega, the Barun Valley, Dudh Kosi Valley, Junbesi, Namche Bazar, the Bay of Bengal, the Ganges River, and the Alaknanda River. Share what you learn.

From *The World's Regions and Weather*. © 1996. Teacher Ideas Press. (800) 237-6124.

📖 *Susan Butcher and the Iditarod Trail*

◆
BRIDGES

by Ellen M. Dolan
New York: Walker, 1993. 103p.

Illustrated with black-and-white photographs, this book begins with the history of sled dog racing in Alaska and then follows the life of Susan Butcher, emphasizing her years of racing on the Iditarod Trail since 1978 and including the many awards she has won as an outstanding athlete.

Susan Butcher was born in 1954 in Massachusetts. Susan got her first dog, Cabee, when she was four years old. Her second dog was a Siberian husky named Maganak. She began to attend sled dog races in New Hampshire and bought another husky to be a teammate for Maganak. At about this time, she went to live with her grandmother in Maine.

When Susan was 17, she moved to Boulder, Colorado and began working in a kennel, helping to train and run dogs. She also became an assistant to a veterinarian. In 1975, Susan got a job in Fairbanks, Alaska. She held a variety of jobs, including working in a salmon factory, and saved enough money to buy a dog team.

In 1978, Susan Butcher ran her first race. The book details the many trials she endured during the 1982 Iditarod Trail Sled Dog Race. She placed second, just three and one-half minutes behind the winner, Rick Swenson. In 1986, Susan Butcher finally won the Iditarod.

Possible Topics for Further Investigation

1 A sled dog race as big as the Iditarod requires all kinds of support services. One service mentioned in this book is the work of volunteer ham radio operators at each of the 21 check points. These hams bring and set up their own equipment, and they must be able to bounce beams along the trail to maintain constant communication between the checkpoints. They know when each musher has left a specific checkpoint and whether anyone is overdue. Ham operators provide all kinds of interesting services in the lower 48 states too. Locate a ham radio operator in your community. Invite that person to come to your class and to bring along equipment. Arrange for a time for the ham to discuss amateur radio with your classmates.

2 One of the awards given at the Iditarod Race each year is the Leonhard Seppala Humanitarian Award, which is given to the musher who, according to the race veterinarian, has taken the best care of the dogs on the trail. Do some research to find out more about Leonhard Seppala. Write a short paper detailing what you learn. Be sure to cite the sources of your information.

3 This book describes what happens when a team pulls into a checkpoint along the Iditarod Trail. Imagine that you have entered the race following the northern route. It is 93 miles from Rohn to Nikolai. Make an entry in your diary telling about your trip so far and the various things you have done at the checkpoint to care for your dogs before taking this short rest for yourself. Share your diary entry with your classmates.

Nonfiction Connections

The Conquest of Everest

by Mike Rosen
New York: Bookwright Press, 1990. 32p.

This large-format, easy-to-read book is illustrated with drawings and black-and-white and color photographs. It is part of a series of books on great journeys and provides an interesting introduction to Mount Everest, located in the Himalayas.

The book is divided into 13 chapters, beginning with the challenges represented by undertaking a climb of this great mountain. It then goes through various expeditions, from early attempts to the 1953 expedition when Tenzing Norgay and Edmund Hillary became the first to reach the summit. Sections are devoted to women on Everest, the various faces of the mountain, and the "unclimbed ridge."

Part of the charm of this book lies in its early photographs of such groups as George Mallory's 1921 expedition and the oxygen equipment used in 1922, and in comparing the articles in these pictures with modern dress and equipment.

Considerable detail about the 1953 attempts is given. On May 27th, Charles Evans and Tom Bourdillon came within 300 feet of the summit before developing a problem with oxygen. They returned to camp. Hillary and Norgay were chosen to make a second attempt. To avoid cornices, they crossed a dangerous, long, smooth slope, discovered what is now called Hillary's Chimney, and struggled to the summit.

Possible Topics for Further Investigation

1 If there is a mountaineering shop or club located in your community or nearby, call or write to try to arrange for a climber to visit your class. Ask the climber to discuss the training and experience that are necessary before a person undertakes a climbing expedition. If possible, have the climber bring in various pieces of equipment and examples of the supplies that are used for the climb and for staying at a base camp. If the climber has pictures of mountains he or she has climbed, ask if they can be shared. Examples of snow/mountain sporting clubs:

Appalachian Mountain Club
5 Joy Street
Boston, MA 02108

The Mountaineers
300 Third Avenue West
Seattle, WA 98119

Adirondack Mountain Club
172 Ridge Street
Glens Falls, NY 12801

Potomac Appalachian Trail Club
1718 N Street, NW
Washington, DC 20036

2 Few people have reached the top of Mount Everest. These people have come from a variety of different countries. Design and create a chart showing each year and the number of attempts made, the number of people in each party making the attempt, the countries represented by climbers, the number of deaths, and the number of climbers actually reaching the top of the mountain. Display your completed chart in class. Also share the sources you used for the data you included.

3 The summit of Mount Everest is 8,848 meters (29,000 ft.) above sea level. How are heights of mountains taken? What are the dozen highest mountains in the world? Where are they located? What is the highest mountain in your state? What is the highest mountain in the United States? Use a map of the world and flagged pins to show where these various mountains are located.

Racing Sled Dogs: An Original North American Sport

by Michael Cooper
New York: Clarion Books, 1988. 73p.

This is an easy-to-read book filled with black-and-white photographs. It provides an introduction to the fields of amateur and professional sled dog racing and begins with a discussion of the most famous of all the sled dog races, the Iditarod Trail International Sled Dog Race. It details some of the problems endured by Libby Riddles, the first woman to win the Iditarod, during the 1985 race, such as making a wrong turn, having to replace a sled brake, being pulled face-first through the snow by a runaway dog team, and having the race delayed for several days by a gigantic storm.

The use of the Iditarod Trail in 1925 for a relay of sled dog teams to deliver serum needed to save the citizens of Nome from a deadly epidemic of diphtheria is detailed. Then the author looks back to the origins of sled dog racing and includes some interesting historical photographs. The Nome Kennel Club was organized to sponsor the first All Alaska Sweepstakes Race in 1908, in which 10 teams raced 408 miles. Fairbanks organized the Signal Corps Trophy Race in 1927, and in 1936 hosted the first open North American Championship Sled Dog Race. The book also discusses sled dog racing in Montana, Idaho, Wyoming, Utah, northern California, and New Hampshire. Finally, a section of the book discusses the various breeds of dogs that are used for sled racing and their training.

Possible Topics for Further Investigation

1 Many people in your class will have heard of the Iditarod Trail International Sled Dog Race. The starting point of the race varies slightly each year depending on the snow pack, but the course is generally the same. Use a large map of Alaska to trace the route of the race. Indicate on the map the major towns and rivers near it. Put your map up on a class bulletin board. The race begins each year on the first Saturday in March. If you are studying this unit during that month, be on the lookout for news items about the race. Clip out articles you find and put them on the bulletin board.

2 There are many organizations devoted to dog sled racing, including the Alaska Sled Dog Racing Association, Alberta Sled Dog Association, Great Lakes Sled Dog Association, Iditarod Trail Committee, International Sled Dog Racing Association, Lakes Region Sled Dog Club, Mason-Dixon Sled Dog Racing Association, New England Sled Dog Club, and the Sierra Nevada Dog Drivers. The addresses for each of these groups is included in the book. Write to one of these that interests you. Include a large, self-addressed stamped envelope. Ask for information about sled dog racing. Share the information you receive with your class.

3 There have been many famous sled dog racers, including George Attla and Susan Butcher. Find a biography about a famous racer and read it. In an oral report, share the highlights of your research with your classmates.

From *The World's Regions and Weather*. © 1996. Teacher Ideas Press. (800) 237-6124.

📖 *Snow: Causes and Effects*

NONFICTION CONNECTIONS

by Philip Steele
New York: Franklin Watts, 1991. 32 p.

This is a large-format, easy-to-read book with a balance of text and color photographs. It is part of a series, Weather Watch, that includes information about weather forecasting and the ways in which plants and animals change their behavior according to weather conditions. The book points out that 23 percent of the surface of the Earth is covered by snow either permanently or temporarily. Snow is presented as a part of the water cycle, which is essential to life on Earth. Simple terms such as *blizzard*, *thaw*, *drifts*, *wind chill*, and *ice crystals* are defined.

A chapter is devoted to seasons and climates, with an explanation of the way seasonal changes are caused by a tilt in the Earth as it moves around the Sun. The text explains that our coldest region is Antarctica, where temperatures seldom rise above zero degrees Centigrade. The lowest temperature ever recorded on Earth, -127 degrees Fahrenheit in 1983, was in Antarctica.

Weather signs and forecasting weather are discussed, as are special features, such as glaciers that cut U-shaped valleys, and avalanches that pose a danger to people and buildings. Sections of the book also discuss adaptations of animals that live in the snow, ways in which humans adapt, snow sports such as skiing, transportation in snowy areas, and the special work of snow rescue teams.

Possible Topics for Further Investigation

1   Page 12 of the text suggests an activity that you might wish to carry out for your class. Ask to use a small section of the bulletin board for a month during the winter. Choose cities of interest throughout the world and post the weather for each, as listed in your newspaper, during the month. How cold was it and how often did it snow in these selected cities? What were the average high and low temperatures? How does the weather in the key cities compare with the weather in your own home town?

2   You can use your refrigerator to carry out some simple experiments to share with your class. Pour ordinary tap water into an ice cube tray. Pour ordinary tap water into which a teaspoon full of salt has been dissolved into another ice cube tray. Put the trays in the freezer and check them frequently. How long does it take the ordinary water to freeze, and how long does it take water with salt to freeze? Can you explain the difference and why salt is sometimes sprinkled on snowy roads?

3   A special problem faced by people who travel in the snow is snow blindness, which can occur when eyes are exposed to white snow for a long time. Invite to your classroom an optometrist who can discuss eyes and the protection that they need in both snow and sun. If possible, have a model of the eye available that can be used in the discussion. Be sure to follow up this visit with a thank-you letter to the speaker.

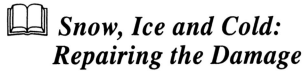 *Snow, Ice and Cold: Repairing the Damage*

by Bernard Stonehouse
New York: New Discovery Books, 1992. 45 p.

This large-format book is filled with beautiful color photographs. Its premise is that while we cannot change world weather patterns dramatically, there are way of improving our efficiency in preventing damage from snow, ice, and cold and in learning survival skills. The chapter called "Arctic Adventure" describes the journey of a band of Vikings who sailed from Iceland to Greenland, their early villages, and the shipping links between Greenland, Iceland, and Norway (roughly A.D. 800 to 1050). After 200 years of settlement, a climate change seems to have occurred, and the villages emptied. Now the Arctic fringe has warmed slightly and is inhabited by Inuits.

The chapter on "Polar Challenge" discusses the hardships of various explorers in the South and North polar regions: Captain Robert Scott on the British National Antarctic Expedition; the Norwegians under Roald Amundsen; and Robert Swan, who led a multicountry expedition to the North Pole. Another chapter is devoted to travel hazards using skis, snow shoes, sledges, dog sleds, engine-powered vehicles, and different kinds of aircraft.

The problems of travel through the water because of ice at sea are discussed. Examples include the difficulties of the Russian cruise liner *Maxim Gorky* and the sinking of the *Titanic*. Whalers and icebreakers are also mentioned. The final chapters discuss snow on the move and ways in which people and animals adapt to being out in the cold.

Possible Topics for Further Investigation

1 Each of the polar expeditions has had a great deal of information written about it. Choose one that is of interest to you and do some research. What was the purpose of the expedition? Who sponsored it? How many people went, and who was the leader? What were the main problems encountered? What special clothing, equipment, or supplies did they have with them? Did these explorers survive? What was their main accomplishment? After you have completed your research, present an oral report to the class.

2 Your assignment as a newspaper reporter is to join a helicopter pilot who will be rescuing people from the ice after the Russian cruise liner *Maxim Gorky* hit an ice floe in June 1989 and the passengers and crew were ordered overboard. Read about this event and then write your newspaper account. You may include some fictional statements from imaginary passengers, but the basis of your article should be factual. Share your finished article with the class.

3 In the book is a dramatic picture of the *Endurance*, Ernest Shackleton's ship, which became caught in ice. There are other descriptions of many different ships from a variety of countries that were sunk after being trapped in ice. Choose one of these mishaps and use it as the basis of a drawing or painting called "Trapped in the Ice" or an epic poem of the same title. When it is complete, share your work with the class.

📖 *Snowflakes*

by Joan Sugarman
Boston: Little, Brown, 1985. 53 p.

This easy-to-read book describes how the many varieties of snow crystals, which we call snowflakes, are formed. It is illustrated with detailed pen-and-ink drawings.

People have always been fascinated with snowflakes and have tried to learn more about them. The text explains that snowflakes are made of ice crystals. Up where the air is very cold, water vapor forms clouds. In the clouds, moving bits of dust become the nuclei around which water droplets collect into solid ice particles. From these particles, snowflake crystals form. Snowflakes may form in any cloud that is colder than 32 degrees Fahrenheit, but snowflakes from cirrus clouds seldom make it to the ground. More typically, a snowflake from a lower cumulus cloud will float down to Earth.

Depending on the temperature, snowflakes form in several different shapes. Scientists have categorized snowflakes by dividing them into groups based on these shapes. The established international classification system includes hexagonal plates, stellar crystals, hexagonal columns, needles, spatial dendrites, capped columns, and irregular crystals. Snowflakes may also change their shapes as they fall through the air. On very cold mornings when there is a low fog, tiny ice prisms called "diamond dust" can be seen.

Possible Topics for Further Investigation

1   This book opens with a poem, "Snowflakes," written by David McCord. There are many other poems about snow, sledding, skiing, snowmen, and snowflakes. You might want to collect a number of these poems and copy them. Then you can display them on a classroom bulletin board. Save a section of the board for original poems written by you and your classmates. Encourage members of the class to contribute their original poems to complete this bulletin board. Save another small section of the board to display the chart explained below.

2   Refer to page 17 of the text. Using it as your main source, make a chart to display in your class. Include the snowflake name, symbol, and examples of shapes of snowflakes that fit within that classification. Add additional columns to your chart to supply the following information: the temperatures at which each type of snowflake forms and in which part of the cloud formation such a snowflake would form.

3   Beginning on page 38, information is given on how to capture a snowflake on a microscopic slide and make a plastic replica of it so you can look at it under a magnifying glass or a microscope. You will need a snowy day, clean glass slides, a wooden slide holder, a plastic spray such as Krylon Crystal Clear #1301, a microscope, and a household freezer. Your science teacher may be willing to help you carry out this activity. Carefully follow the directions given in the text. Share your results with the class.

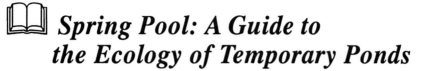 *Spring Pool: A Guide to the Ecology of Temporary Ponds*

NONFICTION CONNECTIONS

by Ann Downer
New York: Franklin Watts, 1992. 57p.

The pool described in this book is located in eastern Massachusetts; there may be some variation in the habitat of pools found in other locations. This beautifully illustrated book is filled with colored photographs and includes bibliographic references and an index.

Spring pools are the result of snow melt and rain. They are usually no more than 3 feet deep and 150 feet across. In the spring, water fills the dry hollows in various fields and woods. The pools become nurseries for amphibians and water insects who mate and deposit eggs in the pool. These creatures include salamanders, wood frogs, and fairy shrimp. The pools are also favorite spots for turtles, herons, raccoons, diving beetles, and dragonflies, who drink and feed at the pools until they dry up in summer. Some pools fill up again in the fall and freeze over as ice-capped pools.

In addition to discussing the life of the pools, the author points out that in many areas such life-supporting pools are endangered for several reasons. For example, acid rain causes acid to build up in the pools and may prevent frog and salamander eggs from hatching. In some cases, the acid rain causes algae to die, and the pool can no longer support life. In other instances, homes, malls, and highways have been built on land that was once home to spring pools.

Possible Topics for Further Investigation

1 If you live in an area where there is a spring pool, you are in a great position to visit it and make observations. You might visit the pool every few days and note what you see. What is living in the pool? Are there animal tracks around it? Can you identify them? Perhaps you can take a specimen of the pond water back to your school science lab. What hatches out? Can you see anything when you look at a drop of the pond water under a microscope?

2 This book contains a section called "Field Guide to Spring Pool Ecology." In it are photographs of the various birds, insects, and animals that frequent such pools. If there is a pool you can visit, make your own field guide. Take photographs of what you see at the pond. Identify the various creatures. You might display your "field guide" on the classroom bulletin board.

3 One interesting section of this book describes how people in various communities throughout the world have worked to establish tunnels so that toads and salamanders that would normally be killed while crossing busy highways would have a way to get to their spring pools. Suppose you lived in such an area and wanted to generate positive public opinion to assist you in having a tunnel put beneath a road. Write an editorial that might be used in a local newspaper. How would you make your appeal? What facts might you use?

Part II
Drought, Dust, and Dunes

Drought, Dust, and Dunes

● FICTION ●

📖 *Canyons Beyond the Sky*
Laurence R. Kittleman

📖 *Dustland*
Virginia Hamilton

📖 *Life in the Desert*
Tres Seymour

📖 *Sandwriter*
Monica Hughes

◆ BRIDGES ◆

📖 *The Dust Bowl: Disaster on the Plains*
Tricia Andryszewski

📖 *Children of the Dust Bowl: The True Story of the School of Weedpatch Camp*
Jerry Stanley

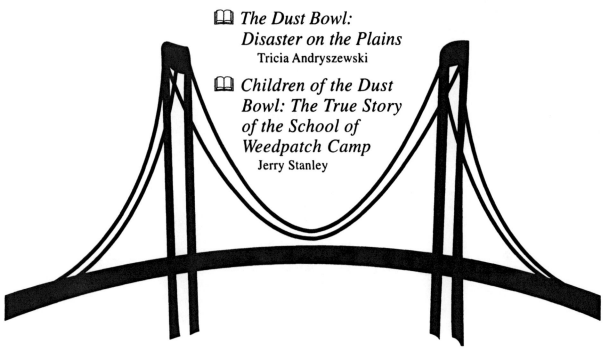

■ NONFICTION CONNECTIONS ■

📖 *Deserts*
Martyn Bramwell

📖 *Deserts and Wastelands*
Dougal Dixon

📖 *Drought*
Christopher Lampton

📖 *Drought*
Gail B. Stewart

📖 *Future Threat or Promise? Deserts of the World*
Jane Werner Watson

📖 *Thunder, Singing Sands, and Other Wonders*
Kenneth Heuer

—OTHER TOPICS TO EXPLORE—

—Farm auctions	—Deforestation	—Mirage	—"Oakies"
—Sand dunes	—Sun blindness	—Oasis	—Sidewinders
—Greenhouse effect	—Foreclosures	—Caravans	—Cacti
—Nomads	—Sand storms	—Camels	—Irrigation
—Sand sculpture			

From *The World's Regions and Weather*. © 1996. Teacher Ideas Press. (800) 237-6124.

Fiction

📖 *Canyons Beyond the Sky*
Laurence R. Kittleman

📖 *Dustland*
Virginia Hamilton

📖 *Life in the Desert*
Tres Seymour

📖 *Sandwriter*
Monica Hughes

📖 *Canyons Beyond the Sky*

FICTION

by Laurence R. Kittleman

New York: Atheneum, 1985. 21p.

Type of Book:

This story is a modern problem-solving adventure tale told in the third person from the point of view of Evan Ferguson. There is a "dream" or supernatural sequence in the story.

Setting:

In and around Antelope Spring, a tent city in a western desert.

Major Characters:

Evan Ferguson, a 12-year-old; his father, Sam Ferguson; Clay Kohler and his son Ceejay; a geologist, Dr. George Foster; and Sheeweklamokun (or Piti), the Indian boy who finds Evan after he falls in the canyon.

Other Books by the Author:

None.

—PLOT SUMMARY—

The story begins with Dr. George Foster driving Evan in a jeep to join his father. They see sagebrush, rabbits, and pronghorns and meet up with a rancher as they cross the desert. Two flat tires force them to camp and wait for someone from Antelope Spring to come looking for them. They make a meal out of a small supply of canned food. Evan cuts his thumb on the can of peaches and comments that he is getting off to a bad start, but George does not seem dismayed.

Evan turns in early and reflects that he is only here because of bad luck. He was to have spent the summer with a friend who developed appendicitis. Because Evan's mother had already planned a trip to Denver, he has been sent to spend the summer with his father and does not feel that he will be welcome.

The next morning, two men in a truck help them fix the flat tires. They then drive on to Antelope Spring, which is nothing more than a small group of tents. They pile Evan's things in the dining tent and go up to the rockshelter. Evan's father hugs him but clearly hasn't given any thought to where Evan will stay while he's here. George finally puts Evan in the storage tent.

George goes off to work, and Evan tries to figure out what the college students are doing with the dirt they are digging up. Evan's father tells him not to bother the workers but to go someplace else to play. Embarrassed, Evan goes off to the creek and then makes his way back to the dining tent. He meets George, who shows him a pool in the creek where he can bathe. Then Evan joins the others for dinner. The next morning he talks to George about the Indian site and what is going on. Then he goes for a hike along the creek. He is back before dinner, but his father scolds him and tells him to stay around the camp from now on.

The next day, Evan arranges things in his tent, carries lunch up to the workers, and tries to make himself useful. While getting George's pack, he skirts the edge of the pit, which gives way, and he takes a tumble. He is not hurt, but his father is angry and tells him to stay away from the digging from now on.

Evan tries to think of something he can do and decides to ask his father if he

40

can go home again and stay there alone. Then Clay arrives with his son, Ceejay, and invites Evan to go horseback riding and fishing on a three-day trip. Evan's dad reluctantly agrees.

Two days later, Evan starts off on his trip with Ceejay. A short distance from the tent city, Ceejay stops and gives Evan some riding lessons. When he's satisfied, the two go on their way again to Aspen Lake, where they unsuccessfully fish and then go swimming. Later, after catching fish and cooking them for dinner, Evan tells Ceejay about his unhappiness at Antelope Spring. For a while they are busy trying to keep the horses calm during a thunder and lightning storm. Then the boys sleep in the tent. The next day, they move on to another lake to do more fishing.

By the time they return to Antelope Spring, Evan has a plan. He goes to his father's tent that night and tries to get permission to go hiking around the camp. His father refuses, but George comes along and offers to teach Evan how to read a map so that he can safely hike in the area. Over the next few days, George gives Evan lessons in map reading. In the second lesson, George explains more about maps and the importance of taking drinking water on hikes and avoiding snakes.

On a hike soon after, Evan becomes hot and comes upon a rattlesnake, but he does well. George tells him he can pick his own spot for hiking the next day but needs to post his destination on the bulletin board. Evan heads for Deadman Canyon, finds a couple of interesting objects that he puts in his pack, and gets scratched up and hurts his shoulder trying to climb up a ledge. However, he manages to retrace his steps and get back to camp on time.

The next day, Evan's shoulder is swollen from his fall, but he cleans up his cuts and stays close to camp.

For several days, Evan hikes around, staying out of the canyons while his shoulder heals. Ceejay rides over to visit him, and one night Ruth, one of the workers, shows things from the day's digging and invites Evan to look. But

Evan's dad comes in and scolds him for bothering people.

Evan continues his hikes and gives what he finds to George. He starts numbering his specimens in the scientific way that George taught him. On Paiute Mesa, he comes across a lot of interesting specimens and takes them back to George, who is excited and asks Evan to take him to the spot the next morning. They have a good day when they go, and George asks Evan to be his assistant; he gets permission from Evan's father to do so. Evan finds that helping George is hard work, but he enjoys it. They see some cairns, and George explains that young Indians may have built them while on "vision quests."

The workers in the rockshelter area find the remains of a house and then human bones. Ruth names the remains "Antelope Boy." Evan is fascinated that this boy, so close to his own age, once lived here about 5,000 years ago. He wonders what the boy might have done. Perhaps he'd gone on a vision quest. Evan decides he wants to go on a vision quest too. A week later, he slips out of camp the night before their day off, when there are no regular meals or events at which someone will notice him missing.

He goes to Paiute Mesa on his vision quest, taking no food or water with him. That night he sleeps near a cairn. The next morning he is getting ready to build his own cairn when he slips and falls over the edge. When he comes to, he is bleeding and in pain. A voice speaks beside him. To his surprise, Evan sees an Indian boy.

The boy says that he is Sheeweklamokun, and he calls Evan by the name of Nehaneepsomokun, Boy-Who-Falls. The boy leads him to a village of huts, where he is kept like a prisoner until he is brought before the elders. Some think that Evan should be killed. He tries to run, but Sheeweklamokun takes hold of him and whispers not to struggle, that someone will help them.

Evan is brought before an old man named Neshi-Zinwa, who says that Evan's spirit has wandered from his body in a vision. They allow Evan to live and send him to gather wood for the fire. Later, Sheeweklamokun takes Evan hunting. Evan stumbles upon Antelope Rockshelter, but there is no sign of his father or the tents. He is very confused and believes that perhaps he is dead and living again in some earlier time.

Evan continues to live in the village and learns about their ways and how to hunt and work with hides. One day Piti (Sheeweklamokun's nickname) tells Evan the legend of Coyote and how he tricked Eagle into forming the canyons where Piti's people live. Piti invites Evan to come and eat with him and his parents. They have a special dinner and that night become "brothers-in-spirit," which gains Evan further acceptance in the tribe. Piti gives Evan a necklace, and later, in a race, Evan wins a necklace that he give to Piti.

Food becomes scarce, so some of the tribe decide to move to the Place of the Hanging Rock, which is another name for Antelope Rockshelter. Piti's family and one other family move with them. They make the move and settle into their new home.

The two boys go hunting for rabbits and scent antelope. They spy the herd and go back to camp to tell the others, who plan to block the exits that the antelope would take and to drive them over the cliff so that there would be plenty of food for winter. Early in the morning, the plan is put into action. During the running of the antelope, a big buck runs right into Piti and breaks his leg. Evan realizes that he has found Antelope Boy. In the days that follow, Evan helps with the meat from the hunt, visits Piti, and watches him die.

Then Evan awakes and finds himself in the spot where he fell. He does not know how long he has been dreaming. When he returns to camp, he finds that no one knew he was missing. Evan cleans himself up and is genuinely glad to see his father. Things are easier between them now; they manage to talk a little to each other.

Then Ceejay appears and asks Evan to go with him to Lone Willow for a couple of days. While the boys are there, Evan tells Ceejay about his accident and about the dream he had. He doesn't know what was real and what was a dream. To settle the matter in his own mind, he investigates the Place of the Willows, where he finds a lot of artifacts that he takes back to camp. His father and George come to see the site. His father is impressed with what he calls a big find. Evan names this spot "The Willows." Evan's father says that, with the new find, they can probably get funding to dig in the canyons again next summer. He asks if Evan wants to come and help. Evan readily agrees and is happy at the relationship he is building with his father. When he packs in preparation for returning to his mother and school, Evan is astonished to discover the necklace of his dream in his backpack.

📖 Discussion Starters 📖

Canyons Beyond the Sky
by Laurence R. Kittleman

1 Evan hopes that once they arrive in Antelope Spring, he will find a small town and "be at home." He'll be able to watch TV, play video games, and do other familiar things. This turns out not to be the case. If you were dropped in a place like Antelope Spring for a summer, what things would you miss most, and why?

2 One piece of advice that Ceejay gives Evan is, "Do something', even if you do it wrong." What do you think of this advice?

3 Although Ceejay's father lets Ceejay take Evan off on a three-day fishing trip and the boys are as well prepared as possible, they still run into some problems. What were those problems? How did the boys handle them? What might have happened that could have turned the trip into a disaster?

4 George, Ruth, and Lucille all seem more interested in Evan and more attuned to his needs than does Evan's father. Why do you think Evan's father is so out of touch with him?

5 Although the men in Piti's tribe seem to be in control and are always respected and fed first, it appears that the women actually make the major decisions, such as when and where to move. The women, however, make it seem that the men are the ones who decide. Discuss this.

6 The language of the native people with whom Evan finds himself is sometimes very crude and sometimes very formal. Look through the text and find some examples of each. What is the effect of having these two kinds of language in use in that tribe? Is it an effective device?

7 Evan's "dream" seems so real that he is not able to separate his dream from his life. Have you ever had a dream that seemed so real that you continued to think about it long after you were awake? Discuss.

8 There is one kind of father-son relationship between Clay and Ceejay, another type between Piti and his father and with his father-friend, and yet another type between Evan and his father and between Evan and George. Discuss these complex relationships.

9 In what ways do you think Evan will be different when he returns to his mother, home, and school? What are the most valuable lessons he has learned over the summer?

10 Make a prediction about what you think might happen the following summer if funding comes through and Evan joins his father in digging in the canyons. Will things go smoothly between them? Will their "find" be significant?

From *The World's Regions and Weather.* © 1996. Teacher Ideas Press. (800) 237-6124.

📖 Multidisciplinary Activities 📖

Canyons Beyond the Sky
by Laurence R. Kittleman

1. The reader never learns exactly where they story takes place. At one point George says that radio reception is poor, but that they sometimes hear broadcasts from Reno and Boise. The setting is someplace in the western deserts and canyons. Do some research. Where are there mesas and canyons such as the one discussed in this story within radio range of Reno and Boise? Decide where you think the story took place. Share your information with the class and point out the setting of the story on a map.

2. Imagine that you are Evan and that you just arrived in Antelope Spring a few days ago. You came by plane, bus, and jeep to reach this deserted spot. Write a letter back to a friend in your home town describing what you found here and what you thought you would be doing for the summer. Describe as carefully as you can the desert and canyon areas and the work of the archaeological dig. You can love or hate the thought of being stuck in this spot for the summer.

3. Many famous artists have depicted the scenery and life in the canyonlands. With the help of a reference librarian, find some books that feature artworks of the west or southwest canyons. From these (or from your own experience if you have been in canyonlands), draw or paint an original canyonlands picture. Work in any medium that you prefer. When your work is complete, share it with your class. You might also want to share pictures by other artists.

 *Dustland*

by Virginia Hamilton
New York: Greenwillow Books, 1980. 180 p.

Type of Book:
This is a fantasy in which four young people with extraordinary powers journey through time into a desolate place they call Dustland.

Setting:
A barren place, somewhere in the future, called Dustland.

Major Characters:
The four members of the unit: Levi and Thomas, who are twins, their sister, Justice, and Dorian, a friend and neighbor. Miacis, a dog-like beast that lives in Dustland, also plays a major role.

Other Books by the Author:
Justice and Her Brothers (New York: Greenwillow Books, 1978), *The Gathering* (New York: Greenwillow Books, 1980), and *M. C. Higgins, the Great* (New York: Macmillan, 1974).

—PLOT SUMMARY—

The unit involved in this time travel story is made up of Thomas, the magician; Dorian, the healer; Justice, the Watcher; and Levi, Thomas's twin brother, who suffers for them all. Justice, the one with the greatest power, is responsible for forming them into a unit so that they can mind-jump into the future. The book begins on the second day that the unit has been on its own time and into the future. Using a technique called "mind-jumping," the four young people leave their bodies and travel to a place in the future that they call Dustland.

Using its mind as a vector, the unit wills up an underground stream and purifies it for drinking water. They remain in Dustland only two days and then mind-jump back to their own time. A few days later, they make a second journey to Dustland. This time they come upon a marvelous creature. As Unit members can tune into one another's thoughts, Justice uses telepathy to let the others know about the she-one who catches a Dawip and eats it in front of the unit. They look at the she-one, which looks

something like a mastiff with wide ears and orange membrane pouches behind its ears that swell and pulsate. Justice calls her Miacis.

Justice strokes Miacis and begins to exchange information with her about The Unit's sense of mission. Miacis is nervous at first and wants to attack them, but she finally calms down and decides that Justice is her master. On their third journey to Dustland, Justice tries to explain to Miacis that "back home" creatures such as her are kept as pets. Miacis can mind-trace but cannot speak like Justice, and begins to try to do this.

By the pool, they find new creatures called worlmas. Thomas tries to kill one, but Dorian heals it. Thomas says you can't tell live worlmas from dead ones anyway, because they all walk around. The dead ones finally get so dried up that they break into pieces. Thomas then uses his magic to create the illusion of cliffs even though they are still in the open on the dusty ground near the pool. At Nolight, Thomas wrenches himself away from the others and leaves. Miacis watches over the others. When they awake, Miacis tells them what happened.

Because Levi doesn't waken, Justice can't leave and hunt for Thomas. Justice knows Thomas must return because the entire unit must be present and hold hands to travel back in time. She sends Miacis to hunt for Thomas. When Miacis gets tired, she makes a hole for herself and rests until morning.

Justice waits for Levi to come back to full consciousness. Levi is not strong, and in the past he has been tormented by Thomas's magic. Because they have traveled to Dustland, Thomas has promised not to hurt Levi, but Thomas cannot always be trusted. Justice worries about Levi and would like to get him home. Then Justice becomes aware that something is tracking them. Dorian knows it is a scout, or Terrij, of the Slakers. Slakers are creatures of Dustland that live in the open in groups of 50 or 60. They have two arms and three legs and communicate by skin impulses. The Terrij of the Slakers comes near them and reaches for Levi, and before Justice can do anything, Levi vanishes.

In the next chapter, Levi is seen running alongside Thomas. Thomas took over Levi's unconscious mind when he broke free of the Unit and left behind an illusion of Levi to fool the others. Now Levi feels exhausted as he runs along.

They watch a spectacular dawn, and Thomas offers to let Levi rest, but Levi protests that if he stops, he will not be able to get going again. As they walk along, they wonder if something happened to their real bodies at home, would whatever part of them is in Dustland simply go "poof"?

Thomas uses his magic to create a clump of rocks where they can rest. He also creates an illusion to slow Miacis down. However, Miacis is blind and doesn't see the illusion, so she continues to track Thomas. Thomas transfers his aura to his brother Levi and then slips away.

Miacis arrives and finds Levi disguised as Thomas. Not far away, the real Thomas watches. Then a huge windstorm, a Roller of Dustland, comes. Thomas

becomes concerned for Levi and tries to reach him as the Rollers loom above him. Then out of it comes Miacis.

Thomas tries to stab Miacis with his bone weapons, but Miacis wraps her forelegs around him. She has learned to speak some words aloud like the humans. The two of them roll about in the wave and go to seek Levi. The Rollers carry the three of them away.

Meanwhile, Justice realizes she was tricked and that Levi is no longer with her. She yells at the Slaker and strikes it. Dorian tries to calm her. Justice becomes The Watcher and tries to communicate with the frightened Terrij. The Terrij, or Dustwalker, grows calm as Justice makes mental contact with it. Justice then transfers her mind within the Dustwalker, the Bambnua, and senses its history.

Justice comes to understand a lot about the Dustwalkers. She realizes that the Bambnua is on a quest to find an end to Dustland and a way out of it. Justice learns that Slakers lay eggs, and that they emerged from deep holes and tunnels where they raised their yuns.

Then Justice asks a mind question, and the Dustwalker becomes aware of her. She feels pain, cannot escape from the Bambnua's mind, and faints. Then the other Slakers come. Justice realizes that she will have to carefully communicate with the Bambnua again and communicates gentle pictures from home, including pools of water and babies.

Finally the Bambnua manages to mind-speak. Justice explains to her about The Unit and how they came to be here. The Bambnua wants a demonstration of the unit's power, so Justice and Dorian combine their strength to levitate the Bambnua. The Bambnua goes up high and flies through the blue sky. She looks as if she will fly to the end of Dustland, but then she curves, tires, and comes back down again.

After the Bambnua lands, the Rollers hit, and Miacis returns with Levi and Thomas. Justice says goodbye to Miacis, and the unit joins hands and begins the Crossover. The Crossover is not without dangers because it contains T'beings, individual mind travelers that failed to hold concentration while mind-jumping from one time to another. The T'beings are trapped in the no-end and no-start between times.

The Unit arrives back home in the present time. It is wet and dark. For a while, Thomas cries. Dorian's mother, Mrs. Jefferson, the Sensitive who helped them discover their powers, comes to meet them. She happily greets them all; only Thomas pulls away from her. She explains that she came down to this spot during the night and found that Thomas and Levi had moved and that the four members of The Unit were no longer holding hands. Mrs. Jefferson pulled them back beneath the tree. She began to worry for their safety. Now that they are back, she helps them one by one to stand and begin moving about again.

Levi is very sick. Thomas puts his hands on Levi's chest and tries to cure him. Then he calls on Dorian and Justice to help. Justice focuses the power of the Watcher, and Dorian administers the healant and lets it flow in rays through Levi. Once Levi is strong, they all go home.

On the way home, Thomas and Justice provide some illusions to shield themselves from passersby so that no one will wonder why they are out on the road at this time of night. Suddenly something swoops down on them. Justice warns the others in time, but Mrs. Jefferson's mind is carried off by a malevolent sweep of something deadly from the future. Then it casts Mrs. Jefferson back to them.

They reflect on this new development and think that maybe Dustland is a prison of some kind, and that this power, whatever it is, does not want the unit disturbing things.

When they get home, Justice, Levi, and Thomas find their mother asleep on the couch and their father asleep in his chair. Justice is sorry to have worried them by being away so long. She knows that her parents accept the fact that their children, in some mysterious way, enter the future.

Their parents are awakened, and Justice allows them to understand everything the unit has just been through. Her mother and father are shocked at the physical changes they see in Justice—her neck is thinner, and her eye sockets are getting larger. They also worry about the power, which Justice, as The Watcher, calls Malevolence and which she says will come again and try to discourage the unit from returning to Dustland.

The family eats a meal together, but Thomas manages to frighten his parents again with his thoughts. He threatens to get whatever he wants by using his illusions. Finally, they all go to bed. When Justice wakes again, Thomas is practicing on his drums and cymbals. Justice wanders about her favorite spots on the property. She is glad to be home again.

That afternoon Thomas takes his drums to the field and begins playing. All the neighborhood boys come. Thomas tells them that he has come up with a new game, called "Dustland" that is a lot like *Dungeons and Dragons*. Then, as they are getting ready to play, Malevolence overwhelms them again. Clearly, it will come every day to make sure that the unit remains in the present.

Mrs. Douglas is delighted that for a month everything seems normal. She even begins to doubt that her children have special powers and thinks perhaps she's been caught up in some sort of mass hysteria. She bakes a cake for the children to eat after the drum session and then falls asleep. When she awakens, she finds her husband bringing in the drums. The children have gone again.

Mrs. Douglas is terrified. She reminds her husband that Justice has a birthday only two days from now. He promises her that the children will be back by then. "They always come back," he reassures her.

📖 Discussion Starters 📖

Dustland
by Virginia Hamilton

1 On the second trip to Dustland, the unit comes upon a she-one that is eating a dawip. There is a description of a she-one, but this initial description is not particularly clear. Each person in the discussion group should make a quick sketch of the she-one and then share it with the others. Discuss the sketches. Are they similar?

2 Go through the argument that Justice has with Thomas in which she reasons that no member of the unit can be hurt in the future because they aren't really there. Does the argument make sense to you?

3 What function does the blindness of Miacis have in the story?

4 Stories with twins are not uncommon, but a story in which one twin has an intense dislike for his younger sister is unusual. Discuss what you consider to be the sources of Thomas's dislike for Justice.

5 Thomas not only hates his sister, but also he is always torturing his brother Levi. Discuss why you think he does this.

6 When Thomas is in the present, he stutters. This is one of the reasons why he won't speak to Mrs. Jefferson—because he thinks she may believe she is "better than he is." Why do you suppose the author gave Thomas a stutter? Why doesn't he stutter when he plays his drums?

7 When Justice uses her powers as The Watcher, she undergoes slight physical changes. Her eye sockets grow larger, and her neck gets thinner. Why do you suppose she undergoes changes when she uses her powers while the boys do not?

8 When Thomas is very pleased with something, he uses the expression "sweet" to describe it. Expressions of approval, like other fads, change often. What are the current words that kids use to describe something they really admire?

9 When Justice arrives back home, she is very glad to be there. But for the first time she wonders if they will always be welcome. What causes Justice to have this doubt?

10 Mr. Douglass promises his wife that the children will be back before Justice's birthday. He says they always return from their trips to the future. Do you think the members of the unit will be back within two days? Why or why not?

From *The World's Regions and Weather*. © 1996. Teacher Ideas Press. (800) 237-6124.

📖 Multidisciplinary Activities 📖

Dustland
by Virginia Hamilton

1 On page 68 of the text, Thomas braces himself against the spectacular beauty of Dustland's dawn. Although Thomas tries to make fun of it, he is caught up in the spectacular color show that occurs, with sparks and rainbows and miraculous lights. Illustrate this scene from the book. You may work in any medium that you choose. See if you can capture in a picture what Virginia Hamilton has captured in words. Share your finished work with the class.

2 In this novel, the author uses a common literary convention to depict the telepathy that the four young people use to communicate with each other. Words spoken aloud are enclosed in quotation marks, while words not spoken but passed from mind to mind are presented in *italics*. This can be a very useful device. Write a short story in which a character's thoughts play a major role. Present those thoughts that are not spoken aloud in italics. Share your original short story with the class.

3 Dust can be a major hazard. It can make people sick, and it can cause delicate machines to malfunction. Do some research on dust. Where it is critical? What techniques do scientists use to eliminate or reduce it? What are some of the major health hazards associated with dust and particulates? What has been done in mining and other industries to reduce the potential danger of dust in the workplace? Report your findings to the class.

From *The World's Regions and Weather.* © 1996. Teacher Ideas Press. (800) 237-6124.

📖 *Life in the Desert*

by Tres Seymour
New York: Orchard Books, 1992. 90 p.

Type of Book:
This is a contemporary story that involves attempted suicide; it is told in the first person from the point of view of a high school student named Rebecca.

Setting:
An unnamed town on the East Coast about an hour's drive from the Atlantic Ocean and in the dunes near a beach house.

Major Characters:
Rebecca Altsheler and Joseph Bell (or O. Z., as he calls himself), two students who are juniors in high school; Maria and Jeremy, Rebecca's Academic Bowl Team friends; Reuben, O. Z.'s brother; and Martin, a boy who tries to date Rebecca.

Other Books by the Author:
None.

—PLOT SUMMARY—

In her high school algebra class, Rebecca notices the thin boy, Joseph, sitting next to her. He is staring at something inside himself. Rebecca is fascinated and sends him a note that says, "Hey, you! Anybody home?" Joseph ignores the first note and the one that Rebecca passes to him the next day. On Monday, Rebecca puts another note on Joseph's knee. This one says, "Earth calling! Earth calling! Come in, please! What are you looking at?" This time Joseph writes, "Sand. O. Z."

As she continues to write notes in class, Rebecca learns more about O. Z. She and O. Z. have the same lunch period, and she sees him in the cafeteria, where he has written into his blank book, "March 8. Clouds in the desert." Rebecca approaches him, but O. Z. closes the book and walks away from her.

Rebecca sits with her friends, Jeremy and Maria, who let her know that another boy, Martin Stewart, has been heard asking about the possibility of getting Rebecca to date him. Martin is blonde, cute, and a member of both the swimming and debate team. Rebecca's friends tell her that O. Z. is a strange loner, but they remember that at the talent show he had amazed the audience with his banjo playing. On Friday, Rebecca exchanges more notes with O. Z. and makes a little progress in learning about him.

One day Rebecca sits next to O. Z. in the cafeteria and begins talking to him. He says he lives in the desert. She makes a joke about Bus 30 going all the way to Arizona, and O. Z. becomes defensive and walks away.

That afternoon, O. Z. ignores Rebecca's note. Then he is absent for a couple of days. Martin appears after English class and invites Rebecca to go for a soda. Martin drives her and several other kids to the mall, where he asks her to go with him to a movie next week. Rebecca agrees.

On Monday, Rebecca finds a note from O. Z. on her desk that asks her to come to the library after school to learn more about his desert. Rebecca goes, and

O. Z. begins to read to her about deserts from the encyclopedia. They are interrupted when Maria runs in to remind Rebecca of an Academic Bowl meeting. The next day, when Rebecca uses a bathroom pass to get out of Spanish, she sees O. Z. near her locker. He has left a note inviting her to go to a movie on Friday. When Martin asks her to go out on Friday, Rebecca declines, saying she already has plans for that night. Maria is furious with her.

On Friday, O. Z. picks up Rebecca in his father's Buick. He drives her to his home to meet his family before they go to the film. His parents brag about him, and his brother Reuben tries to help the couple get away so they can see *Lawrence of Arabia*.

At the movies, O. Z. buys buttered popcorn for Rebecca but gets chocolate-covered raisins for himself because they are the closest things to dates that the concession stand has. The movie begins, and Rebecca is very conscious of the way O. Z. is responding to it. She wants to leave before the ending, but O. Z. refuses to go. By the end of the film, he is crying.

Once they get outside, O. Z. and Rebecca bump into Martin and his date. Rebecca suggests a short drive before going home and asks O. Z. why people at school don't call him Joe, as his parents do. He says he can't help what his parents call him, but that his name is O. Z. Then she asks why he lives in the desert. He responds that his life is a desert, empty and meaningless. He takes her home and, just before he leaves, gives her a little blooming cactus.

On Monday, Martin and his friends surround O. Z. in the cafeteria and cause him to bolt. Rebecca sees this but does not hear what they say to him. She calls him at home and suggests that they meet in the park on Thursday after school. O. Z. agrees.

In the days ahead, O. Z. and Rebecca see a lot of each other. O. Z. takes her to his home and shows her his room, which is decorated in a southwestern motif. While she is there, Reuben manages to have a few words alone with Rebecca and

tells her that she is the first friend O. Z. has ever brought home.

Rebecca and O. Z. have long conversations. Clearly, O. Z. thinks his life is terrible. He asks, "What makes life so damned wonderful if you're miserable? How do you know dead isn't better?" Although it is a tough question, Rebecca argues that you have to stick with life and hope that things will change for the better.

In class, the teacher tries to discourage note writing among her students by reading three notes aloud to embarrass the authors. O. Z.'s note is not among those read. Later, he gives Rebecca a note saying that his family is going to a beach house for the weekend and that she is invited to join them.

Martin tries to date Rebecca again, but she is sharp with him. He wants to know what is so special about O. Z. and suggests that the boy is gay. Rebecca responds angrily.

On Friday, O. Z. and his brother and parents pick up Rebecca. On the drive to the beach house, O. Z.'s parents brag about him and have little to say about Reuben. At dinner, O. Z.'s parents talk about how O. Z. will go to Harvard or Cornell and how Reuben could only get into a state school.

O. Z. disappears into the dunes after dinner. Reuben and Rebecca walk out on the beach, where they sit, and Reuben describes how difficult things are for Joe, who is smart, but nothing he does is ever good enough to suit his father. Reuben is worried about his brother and the pressure he is under.

It is too cold to swim the next morning, so Rebecca and O. Z. decide to go beachcombing and crabbing. As they catch crabs, they talk. O. Z. points out how easy animals have it. Rebecca wonders if they're happy. O. Z. says the question isn't whether they're happy, but whether they know the difference like people do.

They return with 15 crabs and then go out to the boardwalk. It is windy, and O. Z. leads the way into a spot in the dunes. Rebecca realizes at once that this is "the desert" of which O. Z. is always thinking. He has built a magnificent sand castle.

Rebecca asks why he stays in the desert. O. Z. says he stays in the desert because he's safe there and doesn't have to please anyone. He also says that the desert is his future; that's he's not going to be great or famous, but that his future is flat, empty space. Rebecca disagrees with him.

O. Z. pulls his wrapped notebook from the sand castle. He reads a poem written by Percy Bysshe Shelley in 1818 about Ozymandias, King of Kings. He gives her the book to read after she gets home. Rebecca realizes that his name O. Z. must come from the poem.

When Rebecca goes home, her parents have a lot of questions. Then she has homework to do, so she doesn't actually read O. Z.'s notebook until her physical education period, when she sits out, pretending to have cramps. She discovers that the notebook contains mostly short entries. While she reads it, Martin comes and snatches the book and runs into the boys' locker room.

Rebecca waits until all the boys come out. Martin no longer has the book; he has passed it on to someone else. Not knowing what to do, Rebecca hurries to the lunchroom, but O. Z. is not there. Jeremy comes in and tells her to go to O. Z.'s locker to see what a friend of Martin's has written there.

Rebecca runs to O. Z.'s locker and finds written on it in bright red crayon comments such as "may the fleas of a thousand camels infest your armpits." She tries to rub the messages off but has made little headway when O. Z. appears. He feels betrayed and leaves her there.

On her way to algebra, Rebecca meets Martin, who says that he has returned the notebook. O. Z. is not in class. After school, Rebecca phones O. Z.'s home. His mother is distraught: O. Z. has not come home from school, and someone has stolen the family car.

Suspecting what has happened, Rebecca phones Reuben at college. He says he will drive right back and pick her up, and they'll go look for O. Z. He advises her not to tell his parents anything. He gets there quickly and drives them to the beach house. Rebecca asks Reuben to wait while she goes alone to the dunes. There she finds the sand castle wrecked and the notebook abandoned. The boys have scribbled in it. O. Z. has made one last entry that says the desert has been desecrated and the sea is coming and will make an end. She sees his footprints going over the dunes and follows them to the water.

Then she hears Reuben calling. He has found O. Z., who has almost drowned. Rebecca runs to the beach house and phones for an ambulance.

Rebecca is not able to see O. Z., for two weeks. At school, she gets furious with Maria for saying that O. Z. is crazy for trying to kill himself. Rebecca says that O. Z. is her friend and that Maria should never call him crazy again.

When Rebecca does see O. Z. in the hospital, she suggests that next year he join the Academic Bowl. O. Z. says that although nothing has been decided, he may attend another school. He tells her that when he tried to commit suicide he learned that the desert was too horrible to take, and that he would rather stand and wait for things to change.

Before she leaves, O. Z. tells her that his name is Joseph, not Joe or anything else, but Joseph. She respects that and realizes that she is a Desert Dweller too, and that perhaps everybody is.

📖 Discussion Starters 📖

Life in the Desert
by Tres Seymour

1 The letters O. Z. are not the initials of Joseph Bell, but that's what he asks his teachers and others to call him. What did you think these initials stood for when you started reading the book and before you came to the explanation?

2 Rebecca says that although she sat near O. Z. for weeks, she never really noticed him before. Have you ever been in a situation where you were around someone for quite some time before you really noticed that person? If so, what happened to cause you to finally notice?

3 Rebecca's friend Maria is far more interested in having Rebecca go out with Martin than with O. Z. Why do you think that is the case?

4 When Rebecca goes to O. Z.'s house for the first time, everyone is exceptionally friendly, and there is lots of bragging about O. Z.'s accomplishments. Little is said abut his brother. Discuss why you think his parents acted the way they did.

5 The 8-Plex theater is commonly called "God's Theatre" by the kids at school. Why would they give it that name? Has some spot in your community been given an unusual name by kids in town? What is it, and how did it get its name?

6 Discuss why you think Rebecca tried to get O. Z. to leave the theater before *Lawrence of Arabia* ended.

7 Although O. Z. gives Rebecca his notebook on Saturday, she does not read it until Monday during gym class. If you had been given this notebook, would you have waited that long to read it?

8 Rebecca does not want to be called by any short versions of her name. At the end of the book, O. Z. wants to be called Joseph, not by a nickname. By having both the main characters react in similar ways, what does the author achieve?

9 How do you think Rebecca will respond in the weeks ahead to Martin and his buddies?

10 What do you think will happen to Joseph? Will he return to school? Will he ever come out of the desert?

📖 Multidisciplinary Activities 📖

Life in the Desert
by Tres Seymour

1   Early in the book, when O. Z. is in the library trying to explain deserts to Rebecca, he shares some information about life in the desert. He says that those who live there, like the Saharan Bedouins, wander from oasis to oasis. Do some research about Bedouins. Where do they live? How do they get food and water? What sorts of clothing do they wear? Is their life in the desert different today from the way it was hundreds of years ago? If so, how has it changed? If not, why hasn't it changed? Share what you learn with your class.

2   O. Z. reads a poem by Shelley to Rebecca. Find the original poem and do some research about it. When and why was it written? What is the poem about? When you have read and understood the poem, do you think that it is a good one to appear in this book? Who is Ozymandias, King of Kings? When Ozymandias said, "Look on my Works, ye Mighty, and despair!" what is meant? Write a short paper in which you discuss this poem and its meaning. Share it with your class.

3   Suicide, especially teen suicide, appears to be on the increase in the United States. Research this topic and put the data that you find in charts and graphs to share with your class. Compare the reported suicides among different age groups for a number of years. Is teen suicide on the rise? Compare the rates in the United States with those of other parts of the world. How does the United States compare with other countries?

 *Sandwriter*

by Monica Hughes
New York: Henry Holt, 1985. 159 p.

Type of Book:
This book is a fantasy written in the third person from the viewpoint of 17-year-old Princess Antia.

Setting:
Two imaginary kingdoms, Kamalant and Roshan.

Major Characters:
Princess Antia, who is 17 years old; her nurse, Nan; Eskoril, Antia's tutor; Aunt Sankath and Uncle Rangor, Antia's aunt and uncle; Lady Sofi and Chief Hamrab of Roshan; Jodril, their son; Shudi and Atmon, a man and wife who live near an oasis in Roshan; and Sandwriter.

Other Books by the Author:
Beyond the Dark River (New York: Atheneum, 1981), *The Crystal Drop* (New York: Simon & Schuster Books for Young Readers, 1993), and *The Dream Catcher* (New York: Atheneum, 1987).

—PLOT SUMMARY—

Princess Antia is in her garden at Malan with her nurse. She is bored and misses her tutor Eskoril, so she climbs a tree and looks out at the world beyond the castle. A carriage arrives from Roshan, the desert island across the small sea. Out of the carriage steps Eskoril and a woman; they are greeted by Antia's aunt and uncle.

Antia climbs down from the tree, bathes and dresses, and joins her aunt and uncle. She is introduced to Lady Sofi, who, she learns, is the wife of Chief Hamrab, ruler of Roshan. Lady Sofi plans to take Antia back with her to Roshan. Antia guesses that Lady Sofi's visit has something to do with a matter of state and that her aunt is trying to marry her off to the prince of Roshan. She refuses to go to Roshan.

In the next scene, however, Antia and Nan are headed for Roshan in a royal barque. The princess has agreed to go after having a long conversation with Eskoril in which he hinted that if Antia went, his fortunes would change, and perhaps he could approach her as something more than a humble tutor.

Antia is not impressed with Roshan because the city of Lohat has no palace. She meets the chief of Roshan and his son, Jodril, then goes to her bare, plain room to rest, where she rushes off a letter to her aunt and uncle and another to Eskoril.

For the next several days, Antia is taken everywhere by Lady Sofi to see the sights of Roshan. She receives a letter from Eskoril telling her to send letters to him by way of the saddlemaker Berron.

Antia tries to persuade Chief Hamrab to let her go to Monar with the caravan. When he does not immediately grant her wish, Antia asks to be sent home on the next ship. Chief Hamrab relents and says that she may go in a few days and that Jodril will accompany her. Thus, Antia leaves Roshan, riding with Jodril on a *kroklyn*, a huge beast standing taller than a house, with a serpentine neck, hairy legs, and enormous padded feet. She becomes very uncomfortable riding the strange animal and feels that she is on a treadmill going nowhere.

In the evening, they stop. Antia is sore, weary, thirsty, and hungry. She is given her ration of water, some nuts, a bunch of dates, and a cake called *mishli*. She eats and beds down for the night.

The next day they reach the oasis of Arrat. On the afternoon of the fourth day of the desert crossing, the sky gets dark as a dust storm approaches. Jodril moves the six kroklyns into a circle, and the men erect a roof over the center with cloth tied from saddle to saddle. Everyone huddles in the center of the circle. The men begin to mumble, and Antia thinks they are talking about her. They seem to be saying something about the Great Dune being angry. The storm ends, but they remain in this spot for the night.

Jodril points out that there may be a second blow, but Antia goes for a walk anyway. The wind starts up again. Jodril waves at her to return, but Antia sees a huge shape atop a ridge. Instead of returning to Jodril, she goes in search of the figure, but becomes lost and takes shelter near a small shrub.

Antia has several strange experiences. She feels herself held by strong arms, sees flames on a lake, and drinks water. Then she hears a musical note and feels as if she is inside a hollow crystal.

When Antia awakens, she is in a sandstone room, and Jodril is shaking her. She is in an underground house. Jodril cannot understand how she made it to the oasis of Ahman, to which they were headed before the storm. They quarrel.

Shudi, the woman of the house, appears and says that if Antia and Jodril will act like friends, she will be happy to have them eat at her table. Reluctantly, they agree. Shudi says that her husband, Atmon, found Antia slumped against their doorway. They assume that she walked there through the desert.

Antia tells Jodril about seeing the beckoning figure in the desert. He says it must have been a *wrytha*, or ghost. Then they learn that their drivers have left the oasis and gone on to Monar without them. They must wait for their return in this small village of about 10 underground houses near the oasis.

Noticing a large dune not far away, Antia wants to climb it for a look around. Jodril tells her she must come back because the Great Dune is sacred to the desert people. Reluctantly she goes back to the village with him. She returns to Shudi's home and writes in her diary, but Jodril finds it and rips out several pages.

Antia decides to climb the Great Dune. Jodril wants to stop her, but Shudi says to let her go because "only if she is destined for the truth will she be able to see it." She hikes to the Great Dune and writes her name in the sand. Then, as she turns to leave, she sees a strange figure, an old woman who says she is Sandwriter. The woman tells Antia they have met before and will meet again.

On the seventh day, the caravan returns. Antia and Jodril join them and travel back to Lohat. At dinner that night, when asked about her trip, Antia says it was interesting. Antia gets through the dinner by wearing gloves to hide the cuts on her hands that she got from holding the reins of the kroklyn. When she writes Eskoril about her adventures, she does not mention Sandwriter.

A letter arrives from Eskoril. He wants information about the Source. Antia has no idea what she means. She wishes that she could put things right but cannot because she does not know what is going on.

Borrowing clothes from Lady Sofi, Antia goes swimming and riding with Jodril. She writes again to Eskoril and says that she greatly exaggerated her adventures in her last letter. Oddly, an answer comes quickly. The letter contains half threats and half flattery.

During a walk with Jodril, Antia asks him about the Great Dune, the cave, and the pools. Jodril tells her they are not just secrets but the heart and soul of Roshan. Then Antia confesses that she has written of these things to Eskoril. Jodril is very angry and accuses Antia of being a spy. Antia says she realizes now that she was wrong. Then she tells him about meeting Sandwriter. Jodril says they must return home and tell his father all about this.

Antia is called to speak with Chief Hamrab. Then, six days later, she and Jodril return to the oasis of Ahman. That night, they slip away on a kroklyn and go to the Great Dune. They wait until dawn and then walk down to the handar. Jodril puts a basket of fruit as an offering at the base of the handar. The strange woman comes again and leads Jodril and Antia inside the cliff. Using torches, they carefully descend into an area where there is a pool of water. They eat the basket of fruit, and then the strange woman tells them a story:

In the beginning, Rokam was a ball of hot rock. Then it rained for hundreds of years. When it finally stopped, half of Rokam was beneath the sea. What remained were the twin continents of Kamalant and Komilant, the island of Roshan, and the Far Islands in the midst of the Great Sea. Then the first men, three brothers, appeared on Rokam. The oldest claimed the continent of Kamalant. The second brother claimed Komilant. This left the island of Roshan for the youngest brother. The older brothers devised magic to bring rain to their continents, but left little for the island of Roshan.

Seeing that his people were suffering, the youngest brother sought the rain gods in the middle of the desert. Three strange beings came to him. They put water beneath the ground and advised him that if the people of Roshan were careful, there would always be enough water for them. His robe became a pillar, or handar, that allowed him to always locate this spot.

After telling them the story, the Sandwriter takes Jodril and Antia to see the power of Roshan—a pool on which there is fire. Antia realizes that her Aunt Sankath and Eskoril have tricked her and that they are after this power. She and Jodril return to the oasis, and Antia takes a nap. She is awakened by a driver who says she is to go to Jodril back in the valley. Antia sets off with the man but becomes suspicious when he falls back and wants her to lead. She notices that the driver walks with a limp, and she remembers that her tutor also had a limp. Antia knows now that she is in great danger.

She tries to return to the oasis, but the driver twists her arm and says she must take him to the caves. Antia leads him into an opening of the cliff that she knows is just a maze. But the driver uses chalk to mark the way. When they come to a dead end, he follows his chalk mark back out again. She leads him into another false opening, but again the man senses a trap and leads them back out again. Then he forces her to lead the way into the correct opening that leads to the pools. Once inside, Eskoril drops his pretense. He tells Antia of his plans to become the power behind the Queen. If the Queen gives him trouble, Eskoril will arrange for her to die and will then marry Antia and take over the throne.

Antia leads him to the pool of water and tries to convince him that this is the heart of Roshan. But he sees a smudge on her robe from where she had rubbed her hand after touching the oillike methli pool she had been shown earlier. Eskoril insists that she lead him on to the black pool of methli. However, she tricks him into going on through the cave while actually pointing him toward a dead end. She tries to return the way they came, but she gets confused and comes back to the black pool. Sandwriter comes and leads Antia out of the cave.

When they come out, they see a small dot, which is Eskoril making his way back to Monar. Sandwriter assures Antia that he will be stopped. They climb down from the cliff and are met by Jodril. The three of them ride off toward Ahman.

They stop briefly, and Sandwriter climbs up on a dune and calls out to the wind. They continue to the home of Shudi. The Sandwriter, who is old and frail, becomes unconscious. When they arrive at Shudri's house, everyone is getting ready for a great sandstorm. Shutters are being put up, and covers are rigged above the courtyard. Shudri explains that Sandwriter is Jodril's aunt. A beautiful girl, she was called to live with the Old One and to learn all the secrets of Roshan. When the Old One died, she became Sandwriter.

When the storm abates, Antia persuades Jodril and Atmon to let her come with them and to go looking for Eskoril. They find his body and take him back to the village. The next day, Antia talks with Sandwriter, who takes Antia and Jodril back to the Great Dune. They each write their name in the sand.

Sandwriter says that two houses will be united in peace and that a child from that union will come to her. She hopes that she will not have to wait long for this to happen.

📖 Discussion Starters 📖

Sandwriter
by Monica Hughes

1 When Antia's aunt is introduced near the beginning of the book, what initial impressions did you form of her? As you came to know more about her, were your initial impressions correct?

2 Although Antia says she wishes her uncle had more time for her, we never hear her uncle speak. Because he is silent, what impression do you gain of him?

3 The day of their arrival by boat in Roshan, Antia makes a number of comparisons between the country she has left and the land to which she has just come. What are the differences between the two?

4 Lady Sofi explains the secret of life in Roshan: "to bend to the greater force; to bend but not to be broken." Discuss this "secret."

5 Jodril says that Roshan has handars, pillars of sandstone beautifully shaped by the wind gods, that make entrances to the gods' houses. Have you heard other stories or legends about natural phenomena that are associated with the gods?

6 Throughout the book, the expression "a ten-day" is used. This term loosely corresponds to "a week." Why do you suppose the author invented this expression?

7 On page 63, Antia lists some questions in her diary. What literary purpose does the author have for including this list?

8 The Sandwriter says that truth is not always obvious, nor is it always easy. "It takes hard work and sometimes danger to discern the truth." Discuss this notion of truth.

9 The Sandwriter tells Antia a story about the beginning of the world of Rokam. In this story, the first men appear—Antan, Baleter, and Calman. In the desert, Calman meets three strange gods who him the difference between knowledge and wisdom. They say, "Knowledge helps men. . . . Wisdom helps human kind." Discuss.

10 Shudi says that the saddest thing about evil is that it wastes what could have been good. Discuss this thought.

📖 Multidisciplinary Activities 📖

Sandwriter
by Monica Hughes

1 At various times throughout the book, kroklyn are described. Piece together these brief descriptions from the text along with your own ideas about these beasts. Make a drawing of a kroklyn carrying someone from Roshan across the dunes. What do these beasts look like? What are the saddles like? How would the rider be dressed? You may use any medium you wish for your drawing. Share it with the class. Did others picture kroklyn as you did?

2 Although in this fantasy, kroklyn are the animals that Antia and Jodril ride, in the real world the most famous "ships of the desert" are camels. Do some research about camels. What kinds are there? In what areas of the world are they used as beasts of burden? What specialized features make them especially good animals for crossing deserts? How long can they go without water? Do they have any disagreeable features? Share what you learn with your class.

3 Bryce and Zion are national parks where the work of wind on sandstone formations can clearly be seen. Some of these rock formations have been given fanciful names, and stories have been written about them. Locate these parks on a map. Gather some materials from your library or write to these national parks. If you write for information, be sure to include a stamped, self-addressed envelope. Share with your class pictures of some of the most famous rock formations and tell the legends about the formations.

◆ *Bridges* ◆

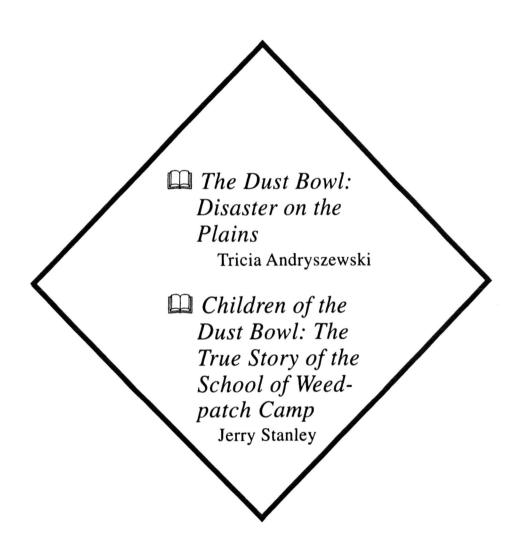

📖 *The Dust Bowl: Disaster on the Plains*
Tricia Andryszewski

📖 *Children of the Dust Bowl: The True Story of the School of Weedpatch Camp*
Jerry Stanley

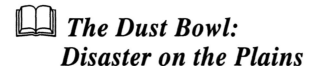

The Dust Bowl: Disaster on the Plains

by Tricia Andryszewski
Brookfield, CT: Millbrook Press, 1993. 64p.

Part of a series called "Spotlight on American History," this book is illustrated with excellent color and black-and-white photographs. Some actual diary entries are included.

The book describes how nature and humans combined to create an area known as the "Dust Bowl," an area that covered 50 million acres of the Great Plains in Oklahoma, Texas, New Mexico, Colorado, and Kansas. The Great Plains was a sea of grass where few trees grew because of the lack of water. Farmers moved onto the Great Plains, stripped off the sod, and plowed up the soil to plant wheat. When prairie fires and overgrazing caused patches of vegetation to die, the dusty soil was picked up by wind. The dust storms began in 1932. Black Sunday—April 14, 1935—brought such a terrible storm that the sun was blotted out and outdoor temperatures dropped by 50 degrees in a few hours. In addition to the dust and drought of the 1930s, farmers also faced the Great Depression.

The book discusses several means used to solve the problems of the Dust Bowl. For example, the federal government bought land and put it in permanent pasture with limited grazing, farmers were paid to use techniques such as contour plowing, and the Civilian Conservation Corps planted millions of trees to help hold the soil in place. Good rain finally came in 1938, and by 1940 the Dust Bowl era was over.

Possible Topics for Further Investigation

1. Once you have read several articles about the Dust Bowl, you might try writing about it as if you were living there in 1935. Write an imaginary letter from your farm in Oklahoma to a friend in New York. Describe the events of one week. Make your writing as vivid as possible, but be sure that the events are accurate. Share your letter with your classmates.

2. This book suggests that a repeat of the Dust Bowl is possible. Frank and Deborah Popper of Rutgers University came up with a unique idea to avoid such a catastrophe. They proposed the creation of an enormous national park, Buffalo Commons, larger than the state of California, giving back much of the prairie to the bison that once lived there. Do some research to find out more about this proposal. Tell your classmates about it and inform them as to whether or not you think this is a good and realistic proposal.

3. The Great Depression and the Dust Bowl made life in the 1930s difficult for many Americans. Franklin Delano Roosevelt was president at that time. His Democratic Party platform included ideas that were part of the New Deal. Many of his programs, such as the CCC (Civilian Conservation Corps), had "alphabet-soup names." Do some research on the New Deal. Choose many of these "alphabet-soup" programs and find out what they were. Design a quiz for your classmates in which students identify as many of the various agencies that came out of the New Deal as possible.

Children of the Dust Bowl: The True Story of the School of Weedpatch Camp

by Jerry Stanley
New York: Crown, 1992. 86p.

This book is a true story about families that left the Dust Bowl and went to live in a farm-labor camp located near the town of Arvin in California's San Joaquin Valley. It is illustrated with black-and-white photographs.

Chapter 1 explains how drought and dust forced nearly 50 percent of the farms in Oklahoma to change hands in bankruptcy court sales in the 1930s. Between 1935 and 1940, more than one million people left their homes in Oklahoma, Texas, Arkansas, and Missouri and moved to California where, according to posted handbills, plenty of jobs were waiting for them. But by the time many arrived in California, all the jobs were taken. People began to live in squatter communities in tents and shacks of cardboard and tin.

The government built camps in the San Joaquin Valley to provide the migrant farmers with emergency shelter. However, Californians treated these migrants badly, and the children were teased unmercifully in school. Leo Hart, who was elected superintendent of education in Kern County, arranged for the creation of an emergency school. Excellent teachers were recruited for Weedpatch School, which was built by volunteers from donated material. They also built a swimming pool. The school and the children attending it thrived. Eventually the school was absorbed into the Vineland School District.

Possible Topics for Further Investigation

Children of the Dust Bowl contains the lyrics of many songs that the "Okies" sang to keep their spirits up on the long journey to California and in the camps where they lived in poverty. Some of these have been recorded, and you may be able to find them and hear some of these songs performed. Compose some simple lyrics and melodies that fit this time and these people. Play, sing and tape record your songs with friends. Share these with members of your class.

1

This book refers many times to a famous novel, *The Grapes of Wrath*, written by John Steinbeck. Steinbeck led a very interesting life. Do some research on this writer and political activist. Write a paper chronicling his life and his most important achievements. Why do you suppose he made people so angry that in some places his book was banned? Be sure to cite your sources of information and to include material from at least four different sources. Share your paper with the class.

2

Choose one or more scenes from *The Grapes of Wrath* to present to your class as a play excerpt or as a dramatic reading. Think about which scene or combination of scenes might make a good 10- to 15-minute presentation. Some costumes and simple props will add a great deal to the mood of your play. You might want to prepare a simple printed program giving a brief introduction to the scene and listing the names of classmates who will play or read each part.

3

■ *Nonfiction Connections* ■

📖 *Deserts*
   Martyn Bramwell

📖 *Deserts and Wastelands*
   Dougal Dixon

📖 *Drought*
   Christopher Lampton

📖 *Drought*
   Gail B. Stewart

📖 *Future Threat or Promise?*
   Deserts of the World
   Jane Werner Watson

📖 *Thunder, Singing Sands,*
   and Other Wonders
   Kenneth Heuer

 *Deserts*

by Martyn Bramwell
New York: Franklin Watts, 1987. 32p.

This is a short, easy-to-read book illustrated with drawings and color photographs. It is a volume from the Earth Science Library series, which explores the world of physical geography.

The book begins with an introduction to arid lands, showing 11 major areas throughout the world where deserts are located. The text describes how nearly a quarter of the Earth's surface receives less than 50 cm. (20 inches) of rain a year and is classified as arid. Of these arid lands, half have less than 25 cm. or 10 inches of rain in a year and are classified as deserts.

Four different types of sand dunes are described, and there is an explanation of how the sands move across the land, as well as discussion of desert erosion due to the scouring effect of running water that carries sand and stones, and of the ways in which minerals dissolve in slightly acidic water. The power of wind in shaping a desert landscape is also explored. Included are photographs of strangely shaped rocks. Plants and animals that can survive in desert conditions are introduced, including aloe and various kinds of cacti, kangaroo rats, gila monsters, camels, and the fennec fox. Desert birds and their means of adaptation are considered. The book concludes with a section on desert towns and ways in which technology is involved in those areas rich in mineral deposits such as gold, diamonds, phosphates, and oil.

Possible Topics for Further Investigation

1   This book describes four main types of sand dunes: *transverse dunes, barchans, seif dunes,* and *star dunes.* Study these four types until you are thoroughly familiar with them. Be able to describe the differences in the way they look and how winds create these different types of sand dunes. Make pictures showing each type of sand dune. Explain how each is formed and how you can distinguish one from the other. Share this information with your classmates.

2   Using a large aquarium, you can create a miniature desert habitat in your classroom. Use a variety of books to learn how to set up a desert terrarium. If possible, ask a local expert to help you in planning this habitat. What plants will survive? What layers of sand or soil will you put down? Will any animals live here? How much water should you supply? Do you need lamps for artificial light and heat?
    Set up your desert habitat with a live creature and plants. Plan with your classmates to maintain this desert habitat for a period of several weeks.

3   The world's 11 major desert areas are indicated on a map in this book. On a bulletin board map, share with your classmates where each of these deserts is located. These desert areas differ from one another in many ways. Concentrate on rainfall. In each desert area you have located on your bulletin board, include a card giving the name of the desert, the amount of annual rainfall in inches, and two other interesting facts.

📖 *Deserts and Wastelands*

NONFICTION CONNECTIONS

by Dougal Dixon
New York: Franklin Watts, 1984. 38p.

This large-format book is illustrated with drawings and color photographs. As a picture atlas, it emphasizes the geographic location of the various wastelands in the world, including hot and cold deserts in North and South America, Africa, northern and southern Asia, Australia, the Arctic, and Antarctica.

The book points out that sandy deserts only occupy a small proportion of the desert areas of the world. Many deserts are rocky; some are covered in salt or clay. Even the polar areas are regarded as desert wastelands because of their hostility to life. But the hot desert areas are not empty. Seeds and tiny plants wait for water, and small animals come out at night. Five percent of the world's population live in desert areas.

After defining a desert as an area with less than 12 inches of rain per year (most of which falls in a few days), the text goes on to describe different kinds of desert areas and their varied landscapes. Sections are devoted to the wildlife of the desert and the people who live in these areas and the sorts of adaptations they make to live there.

The final chapter of the book is devoted to the future of the environment. As other areas, such as woodlands and tropical rainforests, are shrinking, the world's deserts and wastelands are growing. The Sahara Desert, for example, is advancing at the rate of 330 feet a year. Overgrazing is one reason for the growth of desert areas.

Possible Topics for Further Investigation

1 Very unusual animals live in desert regions. Choose some that seem interesting to you. Find pictures of these animals, or make sketches, and prepare a bulletin board display for your classroom. Put the pictures of the animals in a circle around a large map of the world. Use a pin and colored yarn going from the picture of the animal to the desert area to show where it is found. Beneath each picture, write a paragraph containing some interesting facts about the animal. If other classmates are interested in the plant life of the desert, they could identify some of the special plants of the desert on your bulletin board.

2 Heating and cooling of air is important in desert regions. Perhaps you would like to try an experiment that shows what happens to air when it is heated or cooled. Place a rubber balloon over the neck of a soda pop bottle. Put the bottle in a pan of water and heat the water. What happens to the balloon? Take the bottle out of the hot water and let it cool. When happens? Explain to the class what is happening in your experiment.

3 The most ancient people who lived in the Great American Desert were the Pueblo Indians of Arizona and New Mexico. These people had special kinds of homes suited for their life in this arid area. They also raised crops such as maize, gourds, and beans and practiced what is known as "floodwater farming." Do some research about the Pueblo Indians. Find or make drawings of their homes. Share the information that you learn with your class.

📖 *Drought*

by Christopher Lampton
Brookfield, CT: Millbrook Press, 1992. 64p.

**NONFICTION
CONNECTIONS**

This easy-to-read book is about half text and half photographs and is part of a series called Disaster books.

One section is devoted to answering the question "What is a drought?" The text points out the differences between small droughts, which many of us have lived through, and major droughts, such as the one that hit the Great Plains of the United States during the 1930s. In that drought, after 15 years of abundant rainfall in an area known as the breadbasket of our country because of the huge amounts of grain grown there, the rains stopped falling. Crops failed, and many farmers abandoned their homes.

Another section of the book describes droughts from earlier times in many different sections of the world, including droughts in India (1769–1770 and 1865–1866). It is estimated that each of these droughts killed 10 million people. China also suffered a terrible drought from 1876 to 1879. The Sahel in Africa is another area that has had numerous droughts.

There is a detailed section in the book on the hydrologic cycle, which repeats itself over and over and keeps water continuously moving. When this cycle is interrupted, the supply of water in an area can start to dry up. High pressure systems, ocean currents, and jet streams with their various effects on weather are discussed. There are also sections on prehistoric droughts and on predicting droughts.

Possible Topics for Further Investigation

1. Many of the books that deal with the topic of drought include numerous photographs showing black blizzards of dust, farm houses and fences half-buried in the dirt, and families that had packed up their possessions and were leaving to find a better place to live and farm. If you are an artist, you will enjoy studying some of these photographs that capture the feel of the Dust Bowl. Make your own picture, using any medium that you prefer, capturing some scene from the Dust Bowl. Give your drawing a title, and put it up on a class bulletin board.

2. Ballads are songs that often tell sad stories. Once you've read about the Dust Bowl, write a ballad that tells about some of the pain and suffering during this time. You might write an original verse to a melody that you already know, or you may compose original music to go with your verse. Either way, record your ballad on a tape recorder and play it for your class.

3. Many things affect weather and determine when and where rain will fall, including the jet stream and water currents. Find out more about jet streams and the unusual currents in the Pacific Ocean along the equator known as El Niño and La Niña. How do these two currents affect the weather? In some areas, such as southeast Asia, summer winds (monsoons) carry moist air inland. In other areas, mountains play a large role, with rain falling on the windward side. After study and research, write a paper on the things you have learned to share with your class.

 *Drought*

NONFICTION
CONNECTIONS

by Gail B. Stewart
New York: Crestwood House, 1990. 48p.

This is a short, straightforward book that is illustrated with color photographs. It is part of the series Earth Alert.

Drought is one of many natural disasters; its effects have been felt all over the world. Drought is not simply the lack of rain, for some parts of the world receive much more rain than others. Drought occurs when an area does not get its normal amount of rainfall over a long period of time. A section of this book traces droughts throughout history, beginning with those mentioned in the Bible and continuing with the 1767 drought of India, China's drought of 1876–1879, the drought in the Soviet Union in 1921, and the drought on the Great Plains of the United States in the 1930s.

A section of this book discusses how some grasshoppers thrive on drought conditions and how swarms of these insects cause a tremendous amount of crop damage when the drought finally ends and things begin to grow again. Because drought and crop loss cause human suffering across the globe, a portion of this book is devoted to answer the question "Can anything be done about drought?" One controversial approach to the problem, cloud seeding, is discussed. Irrigation projects, groundwater reserves, improving farming methods, and stockpiling food for use in times of famine are also mentioned.

Possible Topics for Further Investigation

1 Swarms of locusts have caused a tremendous amount of crop loss throughout the world. Research this topic. What is a locust? How does it differ from other grasshoppers? Where were some of the most famous plagues of locusts throughout the world? When did these occur? What was the amount of damage that they caused? When and where was the most famous locust attack in the United States? Prepare a report on this topic that you can share with your classmates.

2 Drought often causes famine. During the twentieth century, many groups, such as Food First, have sprung up to address the problems of world famine. Find out something about these organizations. Pick one that seems interesting to you. Write a letter to this group explaining that you are studying droughts and famines, and ask if there are materials available that they could share. Be sure to include a large, self-addressed stamped envelope so they can send you a list of available materials or other correspondence. If films, pamphlets, or other inexpensive materials are available, share these with your class.

3 "Black Blizzards" are prairie storms made of blowing dust, several thousand feet high. There are accounts of people who lived through these in our Great Plains during the Dust Bowl years in the 1930s. Write a trilogy of poems inspired by drought. Title one of these poems "The Black Blizzard." Share your poetry with your class.

 *Future Threat or Promise?*
Deserts of the World

NONFICTION
CONNECTIONS

by Jane Werner Watson
New York, NY: Philomel Books, 1981. 128p.

This information-packed book is illustrated with both black-and-white and color photographs as well as with diagrams and maps. It explores the nature of deserts and tells how people affect and have been affected by them.

Because we have a rapidly growing world population, food supplies are increasingly important. But much of Earth's available fertile land is being turned into desert areas. Known as desertification, this process is widespread in India, the American southwest, and North Africa's Sahara Desert. The author sees it as an international problem and believes that in some areas it could lead to famine.

In addition to defining deserts and indicating where the Earth's major deserts are, how they have developed, and how they are continuing to develop, the author also explores various steps that scientists are taking to "green" the world's desert border areas through irrigation and dams. Some students will find especially interesting the chapter on how animals and plants of the desert adapt to their habitat.

There are also discussions of desalination and the use of natural products from the desert as new sources of food and energy. Among the underground treasures discussed are borax, copper, oil-bearing shale, silver, lead, coal, and iron.

Possible Topics for Further Investigation

1. You might want to prepare as a classroom display a large world map similar to the one shown on pages 20 and 21 of this book to indicate where the world's deserts are located. You will show that most of the deserts touch the limits of the tropical zone, known as the Tropics of Cancer and Capricorn. On your map, list the continents and the names of the major deserts as well as the Tropics of Cancer and Capricorn. Use arrows to indicate the prevailing winds. In planning to share your display, be prepared to tell your classmates the factors that are involved in determining where deserts are located.

2. Many plants and animals have special adaptations so that they can survive in the desert. Do some research on this topic and choose some of the more interesting adaptations as topics to report to your class. You might consider any combination of the following: plants like palo verde, barrel cactus, giant saguaro cactus, or baobab trees, or the adaption of various insects, birds, and animals such as great ostriches, cactus wrens, burrowing owls, the desert tortoise, pocket mice, ground squirrels, pack rats, jerboas or gerbils, and coatimundis.

3. Chapter 8 discusses some of the problems of irrigation and mentions many of the side effects of the construction of Egypt's Aswan High Dam between 1960 and 1968. Read the text and do further research to find out more about these undesirable side effects. Report what you learn to your class. Be sure to cite the various sources of your information.

📖 *Thunder, Singing Sands, and Other Wonders*

by Kenneth Heuer
New York: Dodd, Mead, 1981. 126p.

This is an unusual book that deals with atmospheric acoustics. It concerns sounds of meteorological origin. The easy-to-read text is illustrated with black-and-white photographs.

Although this book might be used with any of the four sections under consideration in this volume, it is chapter 11, "Roar of the Tornado and Song of the Sands," that is of particular interest to those studying about drought, dust, and dunes. The author states that the so-called "song of the sands" is the result of discoveries of accumulations of sand that make musical sounds. This sound-making is associated with sea and fresh-water beaches and with high dunes and sandbanks.

On some beaches, grains of sand are borne up by the waves and then left between the lines of high and low water. When someone walks over these sands, or even strokes them with a hand, these sands will squeak or whistle. Research on this phenomenon was carried out at the singing beach of Manchester, Massachusetts in 1884 by Professor Bolton and Dr. Julien. Other areas where sands make sounds include Gebel Nakous, or the "Mountain of the Bell," in northeast Egypt; Rege-Rawan, or the "Moving Sand," in Afghanistan; the barking sands on the island of Kauai, Hawaii; the booming dunes in southwestern Egypt; and the swelling dunes in North Africa.

Possible Topics for Further Investigation

1 It might be an interesting project to make a tape recording of various natural sounds. You could include the music of katydids as well as of birds, and you may be able to capture the croaking of frogs or the honking of geese at a lake. Try to include a section of sounds in the atmosphere, including the rustling of tree leaves in the wind, the sound of rain splashing in a puddle, and the sound of thunder rumbling through the sky. In making such a tape, you should take careful notes as to where and when you recorded each sound. It might be fun to play this tape for your class and have them guess the cause of each sound.

2 Native Hawaiians have said that the barking sands of Kauai, Hawaii, are due to the spirits of the dead who were buried in the dunes. If you are a mystery fan, this may give you the setting for a spooky short story! Write an original short story in which barking sands play a part. You may have a simple explanation for the barking noises or a supernatural one. Share your finished story with the class.

3 Locate and identify on a world map the various places mentioned in the book where musical sands occur: the "singing beach" at Manchester, Massachusetts; the "Mountain of the Bell" near Tor in the Sinai Peninsula in northeast Egypt; the "Moving Sand" near Kabul in Afghanistan; and the "barking sands" of Kauai, Hawaii.

Part III
Clouds, Rain, and Floods

Clouds, Rain, and Floods

● FICTION ●

📖 *After the Rain*
Norma Fox Mazer

📖 *The Day It Rained Forever: A Story of the Johnstown Flood*
Virginia T. Gross

📖 *No Way Out*
Ivy Ruckman

📖 *The Rain Catchers*
Jean Thesman

◆ BRIDGES ◆

📖 *The Rainforest*
Laura Tangley

📖 *Rain to Dams*
Clint Twist

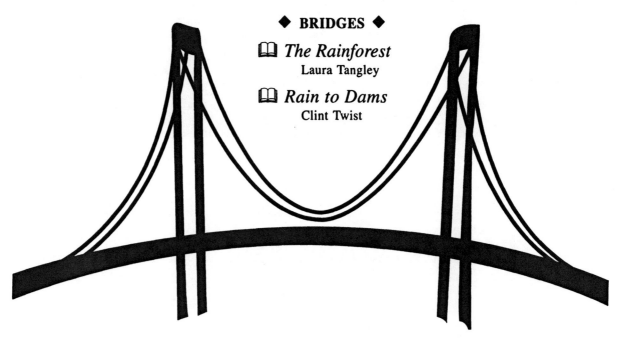

■ NONFICTION CONNECTIONS ■

📖 *Clouds*
Jenny Markert

📖 *Disastrous Floods and Tidal Waves*
Melvin Berger

📖 *Rain: Causes and Effects*
Philip Steele

📖 *The Sierra Club Book of Weatherwisdom*
Vicki McVey

📖 *Storm Alert: Understanding Weather Disasters*
Thomas G. Aylesworth

📖 *Weather*
John Farndon and Marion Dent

—OTHER TOPICS TO EXPLORE—

—Thunderheads	—Dams	—Noah	—Civil Defence
—Barometer	—Canals of Venice	—Cold fronts	—Rain gauge
—The Nile Valley	—Mud slides	—Dew point	—Holland's dikes
—Flash floods	—Cloud seeding		

From *The World's Regions and Weather*. © 1996. Teacher Ideas Press. (800) 237-6124.

● *Fiction* ●

📖 *After the Rain*
Norma Fox Mazer

📖 *The Day It Rained
Forever: A Story
of the Johnstown Flood*
Virginia T. Gross

📖 *No Way Out*
Ivy Ruckman

📖 *The Rain Catchers*
Jean Thesman

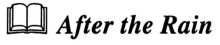 *After the Rain*

by Norma Fox Mazer
New York: William Morrow, 1987. 291p.

 FICTION

Type of Book:
This is a realistic story, told in the third person from the point of view of tenth grader Rachel Cooper.

Setting:
In and near Rachel's home and the apartment of her grandfather, and in Alliance High School.

Major Characters:
Rachel Cooper, 15 years old; her parents, Shirley and Manny; her grandfather, Izzy; her brothers, Phil and Jeremy; her best friend, Helena Minor; Helena's boyfriend, Mikey; and Rachel's boyfriend, Lewis.

Other Books by the Author:
Baby Face (New York: Morrow Junior Books 1990), *Heartbeat* (New York: Bantam Books, 1989), and *Silver* (New York: Morrow Junior Books, 1988).

—PLOT SUMMARY—

The story opens with Rachel, who hopes to be a writer, making notes in her journal. She tears up the pages she has written about her family and begins a required essay on "How I Spent My Summer Vacation." The theme is boring, like her life, and Rachel wonders how she will get through it.

Rachel's mother discusses her grandfather's health. Rachel's father calls her "Mouse," and Rachel reflects on the origins of her nickname. She wishes she had the courage to ask her parents to stop calling her that. Then she explodes at a fairly innocent comment by her mother.

Rachel writes a letter to her brother Jeremy in which she describes problems with her parents; she thinks her problems exist because her parents are old. Rachel finds that writing to her brother is a good way to let off steam, and it seems to help, although he seldom writes back.

Rachel thinks about her family. Jeremy is 35 and brilliant, but he dropped out of college, went to Vietnam for three years, and now works as a waiter in New Orleans. Her oldest brother, Phil, is married and lives in Spokane.

After writing the letter, Rachel goes back downstairs and apologies to her mother. Then she phones her friend Helena, who is dating Mikey, a boy she met last summer when he was a lifeguard at Indian Lake State Park.

In the next scene, Rachel is in the school library during seventh period. She catches the eye of Lewis Olswanger, hoping he will come over and speak to her, but when the bell rings, he darts out without a word.

Once a week, Rachel calls up her Grandpa Izzy, who is a difficult man; it isn't easy to carry on a conversation with him. Jeremy had a tough time with Grandpa on his last visit, because Grandpa criticized Jeremy's lifestyle. Izzy also drove one of his sons to go to London to be an actor. Today Grandpa tells Rachel that he's feeling fine.

Rachel goes with Helena to play paddleball, after which they sit and chat. Rachel talks about how Lewis stared at her in the library. Helena has been talking about Rachel to Mikey and to his cousin, Lewis.

On Sunday, Rachel and her parents go to visit Grandpa Izzy. Rachel walks the few blocks while her parents drive. The visit is dull, with the same questions being asked and answered. After eating, they visit the zoo.

Because Rachel hates to get up in the morning, she always has to rush to school. That Monday, she runs in and crashes into Lewis, sending his books flying. Rachel thinks this may be a romantic moment, but instead feels sick and rushes to the nurse's office. She has the flu.

All week Rachel is home sick. She recovers by the end of the week, but now her grandfather has to see the doctor. The doctor assures them that all the tests are fine, and he sends Izzy home.

At school next week, Rachel keeps bumping into Lewis, but they do not talk. On the weekend, Rachel hopes that this year she will not have to go to hear Gilbert and Sullivan with her father. But she goes, and Lewis is there, sitting only three seats from her. This time they smile and speak.

The next week on Monday evening, Rachel is home alone. Lewis calls and jokes with her for a few minutes. Ten minutes later, the phone rings again—the doctor wants to set an appointment for Rachel's mother to come in and discuss Grandpa Izzy. Soon Lewis calls up again and carries on another funny conversation.

Rachel takes a bus from school the next day and goes with her mother to keep the appointment with Dr. North. The doctor tells them that Izzy has a form of cancer caused by working with asbestos, and he has only two or three more months to live. Dr. North does not think that telling Izzy about his illness would be a good idea.

Rachel returns to school. While interviewing the coach for the school paper, she blurts out that her grandfather is dying. She does the same thing when she meets Helena. At Helena's house, the two girls are joined by Mikey and Lewis. Lewis is almost silent. Rachel makes some sharp remarks to Mikey and goes out into the rain. Lewis follows her, and Rachel tells him her grandfather is dying. On Thursday, the day that Rachel

works in the market after school, she calls Lewis on her break. On Saturday, they go to a movie together.

On Sunday, Rachel and her parents visit Grandpa Izzy as usual and try to pretend nothing is wrong. Just before they go home, it begins to rain again. The next day after school, Rachel gets a call at home. Her grandfather has fallen in the street, and the woman whose house he fell in front of, Alice Farnum, has called for someone to come and get him.

Rachel phones her father twice but only gets his answering machine, so she walks to Mrs. Farnum's house. Her grandfather is there resting. Alice Farnum, a tall, redheaded dancer, mesmerizes both Rachel and Izzy. Izzy insists on walking to his apartment, and Rachel accompanies him.

At home, Rachel tells her parents what happened. They call Dr. North, who suggests that things are moving more quickly than he suspected. He explains that the tumor is pressing against Izzy's lungs, and Izzy fell because he is not getting enough air.

The next day, after an ordinary day at school, Rachel telephones to check on her grandfather. Rachel's parents suggest that Izzy come and stay with them, but he refuses. Rachel calls again and asks him to wait for her tomorrow before he goes on his walk, and he agrees.

Rachel agrees to go with Helena on a ride so that Mikey can show off his Volkswagen bug. Lewis comes along, and the four go to Indian Falls Park, where Lewis and Rachel kiss for the first time. Then Rachel goes to work. Later, her grandfather calls to ask where she was. Clearly, he expects her to come walk with him every day.

All through the next two weeks, Rachel walks with her grandfather after school. She tries to engage him in conversation, but he mostly just grunts. One day it rains so hard they cannot walk, so they play Scrabble. Rachel's mother calls and tells her not to come home until the storm stops. Grandpa Izzy explains that Rachel's mother, just like his wife, is afraid of storms. Grandma Eva used to hide in closets when it stormed.

The next day is a lovely autumn day, but when Rachel arrives at Grandpa Izzy's, he is confused and does not know what time it is. Gradually, their daily walks get shorter. Grandpa can no longer make it up Schuyler Hill. Instead of walking for an hour, he can only go for 20 minutes. But Rachel talks with him now and always kisses him when she arrives and leaves.

Alice Farnum comes to visit. Izzy invites her up to his apartment for refreshments. They talk while Rachel cleans the dishes and dusts the apartment. When Alice leaves, Izzy gives her one of his plants, and they kiss one another goodbye.

One night while her parents are working late, Rachel comes and has dinner with Grandpa Izzy, who does not eat much. He asks Rachel what Doctor North told Rachel's mother. Rachel finally tells her grandfather that he has mesothelioma.

On Saturday, Izzy takes Rachel with him on a bus trip. They go to West Creek Street, where he stops to examine every bridge, looking for his handprint and initials, but he is unable to find them. He explains to Rachel that he was fired from his job for having put his initials there long ago. On another rainy afternoon, she asks to see his photographs. He finally brings out a manila envelope stuffed with pictures and gives her a picture of Grandma Eva when she was about 15.

One night Lewis comes over to Izzy's apartment. When Lewis puts out his hand to shake Izzy's hand, Izzy says that Lewis has a weak hand and would never make it as a stonemason. Lewis is offended but gets over it. Rachel realizes that Izzy is jealous.

Izzy almost falls again on another walk. They have to sit on a bench and then take the bus home. Rachel is slow to tell her parents about this, but as soon as she does, her mother calls Dr. North, who says nothing can be done.

Rachel misses Helena's birthday party because she has to go walk with Izzy. It starts to rain, so they return home. When they get to the apartment, Helena, Mikey, and Lewis are waiting for

them with cake, ice cream, and balloons. Saturday, Rachel visits her grandfather early and they spend the whole day in the sunshine. Izzy seems to be enjoying everything, until, in the afternoon, he suddenly says, "I can't." Rachel manages to get him into a chair in a hardware shop and calls her parents, who come immediately. They take him to his apartment, call the doctor, and then take Izzy to the hospital.

Izzy seems to improve after they remove some fluid from his lungs. Rachel decides to stay out of school Monday and Tuesday to stay with her grandfather in the hospital. On Wednesday, she picks up assignments for the next week so she can go to the hospital every day while her grandfather is there.

Grandpa Izzy grows weaker and constantly needs oxygen. One night Rachel's father stays with him because Izzy is afraid to sleep. On another night, Rachel insists on staying with him. That night he dies.

Relatives gather, and at one point during a family dinner, Rachel, overcome with emotion, goes out in to the kitchen and drinks a glass of water. She has a vision and feels herself walking down a narrow road in the sleeting rain. Later, Rachel's Uncle Leonard calls from England. He regrets not having made up with his father, and he hopes that one day Rachel will come and visit him. Everyone tells a story about Grandpa Izzy, but Rachel merely says that she loved him. They sprinkle his ashes over Grandma Eva's grave and plant a tree in his memory.

Rachel and her brother Jeremy go out walking together. She gets very angry at her grandfather for waiting until the last two months of his life for her to get to know and love him. Her brother tells her that it is bad when you lose someone you love, and he relates this to his experiences in Vietnam.

On a wintry day, Rachel and Lewis go searching for Izzy's handprint and initials on the bridges and finally locate them. After they find the initials, the sun breaks through and feels warm on Rachel's head.

📖 Discussion Starters 📖

After the Rain
by Norma Fox Mazer

1 The first time in the story that Rachel goes out in the rain is on a Sunday when she prefers walking over riding to her Grandpa Izzy's apartment. Why do you think Rachel always prefers to walk rather than ride with her parents?

2 It is raining when Lewis comes with Mikey to Helena's house, and it is still raining when Rachel leaves and Lewis catches up with her. Does the fact that it is raining add anything to this scene?

3 Rachel believes that the major problems she has with her parents are because they are so old. Do you agree with Rachel on this point?

4 Every Sunday seems the same to Rachel. The family goes through a sort of ritual with the same questions and the same answers. Are there routines like this in your family? Discuss.

5 Grandpa Izzy is not a talkative person and usually responds to Rachel in grunts. Gradually, however, she gets him to talk with her. What techniques does Rachel use to get him to open up?

6 Grandpa Izzy tells Rachel about building the wall at the Jewish cemetery and about building bridges over Clearbrook Creek. What does his pride in this work reveal about him?

7 When Rachel learns that Grandpa Izzy left a handprint and one of his initials in a bridge he built, she asks Lewis what he would leave to signify he'd been in this world. What would you leave behind as your "signature to the world"?

8 Rachel is afraid of dogs. One day when she is walking with Grandpa Izzy, a dog frightens her. Even though he is very weak, Grandpa puts his arm around Rachel and protects her. How does this incident enrich the story?

9 Whenever Alice Farnum appears, Grandpa Izzy always perks up. Why do you think she has this effect on him?

10 Rachel has a vision on page 267: With a hard rain falling, she is walking down a narrow, sandy road with large trees on both sides. Interpret this dream.

From *The World's Regions and Weather.* © 1996. Teacher Ideas Press. (800) 237-6124.

📖 Multidisciplinary Activities 📖

After the Rain
by Norma Fox Mazer

1. Grandpa Izzy is very proud of the bridges he helped build as a stonemason. Experimenting with different types of bridges is a lot of fun. Get a long, slender balloon. Blow it up and fasten it like a bridge between the backs of two chairs. Tie a string loosely around the middle of the balloon and allow the ends to hang down. Tie the ends to a large paper clip that you bend open to form an S-shaped hook. Have classmates guess how much weight the balloon will support. Then test your bridge by hooking items of various weights to the paper clip. How much weight did your balloon bridge support?

2. Grandpa Izzy's disease is asbestosis, resulting from his exposure years earlier to asbestos. What is asbestos? How was it commonly used? What are the dangers of asbestos? Some authorities believe that asbestos should be removed from schools and other public buildings. Others believe it should be watched but left in place. Research this topic and report back to the class what you learn.

3. Grandpa Izzy's memorial was an almost invisible set of initials and a handprint on the bridge. Are there some memorials in your town such as statues, parks, old buildings with cornerstones, or a tall monument in a cemetery? Have you ever thought much about the people to whom these memorials were dedicated? Choose one that is not too well known. Research your topic and write a paper about what you learn. Share this with your classmates.

The Day It Rained Forever:
A Story of the Johnstown Flood

by Virginia T. Gross
New York: Viking, 1991. 52p.

FICTION

Type of Book:

This book is part of the Once Upon America Series. It is a work of historical fiction based on the Johnstown flood of 1889 and told in third person from multiple viewpoints, including that of 11-year-old Christina Berwind.

Setting:

Johnstown, Pennsylvania.

Major Characters:

Christina, an 11-year-old; her brother Frederick, aged 15; her younger brother and sister, Herbie and Gretta; her father, George; her mother, Teresa; her uncle, Herbert Berwind and his bride-to-be, Lenora; a family friend, Mr. Koehler; Hope, a baby who was found in the flood; and Mr. Amici, who rescued both the baby and Christina's mother.

Other Books by the Author:

It's Only Goodbye (New York: Viking, 1990) and *The President Is Dead: A Story of the Kennedy Assassination* (New York: Viking, 1993).

—PLOT SUMMARY—

Christina listens to her younger brother and sister playing in the barnyard. They had all attended the Decoration Day parade in Johnstown that morning. Christina is busy stitching a linen towel as a wedding present for her uncle, who is getting married in six days.

It looks like rain, so Papa calls to the children, Herbie and Gretta, to run and close up the loading bay of the barn to prevent the hay from getting wet. Papa and Christina's 15-year-old brother Frederick are visiting on the porch with their neighbor, Isaac Koehler. Christina's mother is in town helping with wedding arrangements. Papa is glad she is there, which keeps her mind off the death of their baby girl Eva only two months ago.

Papa says that they don't need any more rain. Mr. Koehler worries more about the dam up river than the rain. He points out that if the dam gives way, 20 million tons of water will flood the valley.

He fears the destruction of South Fork, Mineral Point, and even Johnstown. Frederick replies that people always worry about the dam, and that there was a wet year last year, but nothing happened. He points out that the earthwork dam is 100 feet high. But Mr. Koehler reminds him that the folks at the South Fork Hunting and Fishing Club shaved off the top of the dam to make a road to please the Pittsburgh millionaires who liked to fish in Lake Conemaugh in the summer.

Mr. Koehler also points out that there are no longer any runoff pipes that would drain off the dam when it gets close to overflowing. There had been five runoff pipes originally, but when the dam was rebuilt, they did not use the services of an engineer and did everything cheaply. They also put a grating over the northern spillway to keep the fish in.

Mr. Koehler starts to leave on his horse to beat the storm home. He asks Papa if Teresa can press his suit before the wedding. Christina offers to do it for him. The rain begins just as Mr. Koehler leaves. Christina and her family go inside and begin their chores. Frederick comments that he'll have to get up early tomorrow and walk to his job pitching coal at the Cambria Iron Works.

The next morning, it is still raining hard. Christina gets up to cook her brother a hot breakfast. She is worried about the possibility of the dam breaking and begs her brother to stay home. Even Papa is worried. He suggests that Frederick should not try to come home after work in the rain, but should stay with his mother over at the bride-to-be's and wait for the rain to stop and for Papa to pick them up in Johnstown. Frederick leaves, and instead of going back to bed, Christina settles on the couch in the kitchen, while Papa goes out to begin his morning chores. The rain continues to pour down.

In town, Lenora Hastings and Christina's mother, Teresa, are busy moving things in Lenora's house from the cellar to the top floor. Lenora comments that this is one wedding week they will never forget. Teresa wonders why Herbert bought a bungalow so close to the Conemaugh river, which floods often.

Upstairs, shortly before noon, the two women look out the window and see Herbert and another man in a boat. Herbert shouts to them that they are moving folks to higher land and will be back to pick up the two women.

Christina keeps busy at home with chores and entertaining her baby brother and sister. She fixes bean soup and biscuits. Papa busily weaves a new cane seat for a kitchen chair. Suddenly Frederick and Mr. Koehler burst into the kitchen. The iron works were shut down for the day, but Frederick only got as far as South Fork, where he helped the sheriff get people to move to higher ground. Frederick says that everyone believes the dam will give way.

Mr. Koehler has more bad news: When men tried to open the spillway of the dam, they could not do it because it was overgrown with weeds and vines. Twenty men had started digging a new channel, which promptly filled with water. Suddenly, everyone feels a trembling and hears a terrible roar. They rush to the edge of the mountain and see the wall of water tearing through the narrow valley. South Fork disappears in the water which races on toward Mineral Point and Johnstown.

Back in Johnstown, the rain continues, and Lenora and Teresa are frightened. They pray close together. Then the wall of water hits them and tears them apart. Teresa bobs up and down in the water, bashing against things, and finally faints. When she comes to, she is caught in the branches of a giant elm.

People, animals, and furniture all go swirling by her. A wooden tub slams into her and wedges in the branches. Then Teresa hears a baby's cry. She sees a newborn infant, wrapped in a soaked blanket, pushing against the side of the tub. Teresa reaches out and, using her apron like a sling, holds the baby against her and pushes the tub away.

The cobbler, Ronaldo Amici, sees Teresa in the tree and hears the baby cry. He gathers a rope and a broom, ties the rope around his waist, and attaches the other end to a spruce tree at the top of the hill. Teresa grabs the broom when the water rises, and he pulls her to high ground just before the elm is swept away.

Teresa awakes, wrapped in a nightshirt and blankets, in Mr. Amici's house. He is feeding the baby, who has a broken arm. He splints the baby's arm and promises to try to take Teresa home tomorrow. Teresa holds the baby close.

Papa and the children wait at home for the water to subside, fearing their mother may have drowned. But to their amazement the next afternoon, Mr. Amici arrives with Teresa and the baby. Although Christina is overjoyed to see her mother, she resents the baby's presence.

Two days pass. The younger children make Christina furious when they suggest that the new baby should be named after Eva. Christina runs in the house. Mama tries to explain that Baby Eva was part of Christina's life very briefly and that this new baby could be part of her life too. She promises that the new baby will not be named Eva. Christina has a hard time understanding, but she tries.

Frederick takes the horse into town to get news. He comes back in two days to report that 2,000 people are dead and many more are missing. Hardly a building was left standing, and people are looting. He explains that many people and objects were trapped against the railroad bridge, where kerosene and oil stoves exploded and started a fire that is still burning. Having helped place bodies, many from the burning pile, on boards across the pews of a church, Frederick is beside himself with grief. Papa pulls down the Bible and reads to his family. Teresa takes the baby and puts her in Frederick's arms. She says they'll name the baby Hope.

After a partial cleanup from the flood, the school reopens for one final week. The adults feel that the children need something routine and familiar to return to. Christina goes to school with Gretta. Their teacher talks to the pupils about how fortunate they are to have survived. One of Christina's friends asks about the new baby. Christina tells the other students about how her mother and the baby survived the flood, and how Mr. Amici is trying to find out if the baby has any kin.

In late summer, Mr. Amici informs the family that in a lawyer's opinion there is no way of locating Hope's family, and that the Berwinds may adopt her. Joyful at the news, Christina takes Hope up the hill to Eva's grave to introduce the two baby sisters to each other. They are joined there by Christina's mother.

📖 Discussion Starters 📖

The Day It Rained Forever: A Story of the Johnstown Flood
by Virginia T. Gross

1   Teresa Berwind wonders why her brother-in-law would buy a house so close to a river that floods. Each year when a town floods in the United States, people from other parts of the country wonder why the residents of the town repair and rebuild and remain. Why do you think people don't abandon a town after a natural disaster?

2   When Herbert Berwind appeared in the boat and says he'll be back later for Lenora and Teresa, did you think the two women would be rescued by him? What made you think the way you did?

3   Papa is a religious man. He is offended when his friend swears and later when Frederick swears. What is the effect on the story of Papa's strong religious beliefs?

4   When you first learned that the dam breaks, did you think that Frederick would be drowned or that he would return to his family? Why did you think the way you did?

5   What remark did Lenora make that gave you a clue that she would not survive the flood?

6   Do you think that you would have resented the baby the way Christina did when she first appeared with Christina's mother? Explain why you think Christina resented the baby so much.

7   Because there was only a week left of school, do you think it was a good idea or a bad idea to open it for just a few days before summer vacation?

8   Why do you think Christina's mother chose the name "Hope" for the baby? If you had been naming that baby, would name would you have given it and why?

9   Discuss why you think Christina took Hope up the hill to the cemetery to the grave of her sister Eva right after Christina learned that her family could adopt Hope. What purpose did this action serve for Christina?

10   There is a brief "about this book" section at the end of the story. Do you think it was valuable to include this? Why or why not?

📖 **Multidisciplinary Activities** 📖

The Day It Rained Forever: A Story of the Johnstown Flood
by Virginia T. Gross

1 In this story, Frederick, who is only 15 years old, works full time at the Cambria Iron Works. Today, such a job would not be open to him. There are many child labor laws that regulate the age of people who can work, how many hours they can work, what their minimum pay can be, and the types of work in which they can be engaged. Find someone in your community who is familiar with child labor laws. Ask that person to visit your class to discuss these laws and to give you a little of the history of the development of these laws. Be sure to write a letter of thanks to your guest speaker afterwards.

2 Dams are often controversial. The Sierra Club and others were very active in protesting the building of the Glen Canyon Dam, which created Lake Powell. With three other members of your class, research this topic. Prepare a debate in which two of you argue for the building of the Glen Canyon Dam and two of you argue against building it. What were the advantages of building it? What were the reasons against building it? Present your debate to the class.

3 This book is illustrated with nine black-and-white sketches. Choose a scene from the book that was not illustrated. Prepare a full-page illustration for that scene using pencil or charcoal. Try to make your picture correspond to the style of Ronald Himler, who did the drawings for the book. Share your new book illustration with the class.

 *No Way Out*

by Ivy Ruckman
New York: Thomas Y. Crowell, 1988. 212p.

Type of Book:
   This is a romantic adventure story, told in the third person from multiple viewpoints.

Setting:
   The Zion Narrows in Utah.

Major Characters:
   Amy, a 19-year-old girl; her boyfriend, Rick Chidester; her younger brother, Ben; a new friend, Clyde McKenzie; Neale, a neighbor girl whose family is also hiking and plans to meet Amy and the others in the Narrows; Audrey and Steve, a couple who are hiking; and another hiker, Gary, who is already known to Amy and Rick.

Other Books by the Author:
   Night of the Twisters (New York: Thomas Y. Crowell, 1984), *This Is Your Captain Speaking* (New York: Walker, 1987), and *The Hunger Scream* (New York: Walker, 1983).

—PLOT SUMMARY—

The story opens on a sunny Labor Day week-end when Amy and her boyfriend Rick are hiking in the Zion Narrows. Amy's brother Ben is with them. They have also hooked up with a solo hiker, Clyde McKenzie. A ranger had suggested that Clyde join their group because he is an inexperienced backpacker, and his hiking companion had come down with the flu. Clyde is happy to be with them. Amy is glad to be with Rick, whom she will marry in a few weeks. She still plans to get her degree in veterinary medicine.

The four take a short rest and then are off again, hiking through the sandstone cliffs to the spot they have picked for their campsite. Then they come upon a rattlesnake. Amy tries to keep Rick from killing the snake, but he smashes it with a huge rock. They continue, expecting to catch up with their neighbors, the Dwyers, with whom they had made plans to meet at the Forks. But they do not see the Dwyers along the way.

Sometimes they have a clear path, but often they have to climb over boulders, scramble up rocks, and get wet in the river. Then Rick frightens all the others by pretending to see another snake. Amy angrily walks off. Clyde walks with her while Rick and Ben rest and eat a candy bar.

Amy and Clyde chat as they walk. Amy tells Clyde about her marriage and school plans. Clyde says he wants to be a storyteller and that his mom is a librarian. The two of them tease each other and have fun together.

Clyde and Amy reach the spot where the North Fork and Deep Creek came together. Neale Dwyer is there, but her parents have gone on to the Grotto, a popular spot for overnights about an hour down the canyon. Two other campers, Audrey and Steve, are also there. Audrey explains that the Dwyers did not want to crowd them, and that Neale was to join up with them later.

The group is in a fix. It is already after six o'clock, and everyone is tired. It will take them another hour or more to reach the Dwyers. Ben complains that he has blisters, while Neale sulks and is uncooperative. Finally they decided to camp where they are and catch up with the others in the morning.

Clyde and Ben decide to spend the night in a cave some distance from the others. Before they go to sleep, Steve discusses what everyone should do if it starts to rain. Then they sing happy birthday to Steve before turning in.

It rains during the night, and Rick wakes Amy. Neale and Amy move up to higher ground. Using a rope, Steve and Rick try to get to Ben and Clyde, but the river is too high and they fail. Steve, Rick, and Amy scramble back up to join Neale and Audrey.

Awakened by the storm, Clyde and Ben try to join the others, but the path they climbed is now covered in water. There is no place to go except up the tree near the cave, so they climb the box elder. A wall of water hits, and trees and boulders come smashing down. Something crashes into Clyde's leg, and he blacks out, but is held against the tree by Ben.

The water in Deep Creek subsides, but North Creek begins to rise. Neale becomes irrational; she has hypothermia. Audrey starts a stove and gives Neale something warm to drink; then they put her in Steven's new wool birthday shirt, and Audrey climbs into a sleeping bag with her, trying to warm her up. They all drink something warm and eat a few of their rations. Then they hear the second wall of water coming. They huddle together, and Steve wraps a rope around them, telling them all to hang on.

Up in the tree, Clyde and Ben worry about the others and themselves. They use a knife to fashion walking sticks. Clyde ties a rope around the tree and drops down to the water.

Amy believes Ben has died in the flood. When Steve thinks it is safe, he goes into the river to look for Ben and Clyde. Rick thinks it is too soon to go into the water, and he is scared, but he agrees to help. They see a flash of red plaid in the river, and Amy falls apart, thinking it is Ben's body. Then they see Clyde. He has made it down the river within shouting distance of them. Amy, Steve, Rick, and Clyde go back to help Ben. They ferry him across and return to their makeshift camp, then get into dry clothes and treat the puncture wound behind Clyde's knee.

While Steve and Rick cut wood, Neale and Clyde go to get water but find that the water supply has dried up. The two begin talking and learn they have some things in common. Neale thinks she will have another chance with her folks if she makes it out of this, but she is scared. Clyde rubs her hands in his.

At the main camp, Amy climbs out of the sleeping bag, furious that it's raining again. Then she sees someone approaching. Amy and Rick recognize this man as a former fraternity brother of Rick's, Gary Rawlings. Weary, he throws himself down at the campfire. Gary explains that he had been with two other guys, but left them when tendonitis gave him so much trouble that he could not go on.

That night, they all gather around a pot of chicken soup. Gary, a devout Mormon, offers a prayer before they eat their meager meal, and Neale sings a ballad. They share sleeping bags, with one person sitting up and tending the fire. Gary and Amy sit by the fire talking. Amy wonders aloud if she should get married. She is not sure after her recent experiences if she and Rick are right for each other.

In the morning, Clyde's leg hurts tremendously. His wound has been oozing all night. Audrey gives him aspirin, and the others decide that Clyde and Gary will start out immediately, because they will move more slowly than the others. The others will follow, and they will meet at the Grotto.

The going is slow for Clyde and Gary. The water is deep, and they have to climb over logjams. When they finally reach the Grotto, it is empty. Then they see a pile of dry clothes, some food, and a note. The note says that 10 people survived and that the survivors are about an hour ahead of them.

The rain starts again. Amy and her party meet up with Gary and Clyde before they reached Big Springs. They worry about whether Neale's folks made it through the next stretch before the rain came, or whether they might not be far away, sitting out the latest storm. They also question whether to go ahead or wait out the rain. They are out of food, and Clyde needs a doctor. Eventually they vote to spend yet another night in the Narrows. That afternoon, another crest of water goes by, and they reflect that if they had left, they might have drowned.

In the evening, Rick goes off alone. When Amy wanders off to find Rick, she discovers that he secretly has granola bars—he has eaten one and has not volunteered to share his food. Amy is furious and makes a scene. Rick is mortified and walks off. Amy sits down, ashamed of him and of herself, and weeps. Later, Rick tries to explain about the food, and Amy apologizes. But things are chilly between them.

The next morning, under sunny skies, they begin hiking out. A plane flies over, and they try to signal it. They continue to Big Springs, where they stop to get fresh water. When Amy and Clyde are partners, walking through the narrow stretch of water, they talk. Amy thanks Clyde for saving Ben. Clyde has decided he and his mother will move out of Santa Monica and go to Eureka, California, where his aunt lives.

They continue though swift, chest-high water. Then their way is blocked by a huge boulder. Steve and Gary try to get across using a rope and hoping to move the others one by one. Steve makes it across. Then Rick joins Steve. Audrey and Amy cross easily, but when it is Clyde's turn, he freezes in terror. Neale joins him and they slowly work their way across. By noon, they are out of the most dangerous section and have only two more miles to go. Clyde is very weak, but they continue.

Amy and Audrey walk as buddies for a while. Amy confesses that there may not be a wedding. Audrey admits that she and Steve are not married, just vacationing together. Audrey's husband has been in a hospital with Huntington's chorea for eight years and no longer knows Audrey. She decides she cannot just leave her husband and move to Seattle with Steve. And Amy realizes that though she loves Rick, she does not love him the way she needs to for marriage.

The group stops to rest. Some park rangers arrive and make a litter for Clyde and Ben. The rangers also share the news that a party of 10 came out yesterday. Neale is happy thinking that her parents have survived. Gary's two friends, joined by his wife and baby, are at the Lodge waiting for news of him.

When the 17 hike out of the Narrows, they are met by news crews and other spectators. Amy's mother and father, Rick's parents, and Neale's parents are there too. Even Jason, the boy who was to have been Clyde's hiking partner, is waiting. Addresses are quickly exchanged, and the group leaves. Two are going to the hospital, while the rest are going home. Amy reflects how strange it is that weak as she is, she comes out incredibly strong from her ordeal in the Narrows.

📖 Discussion Starters 📖

No Way Out
by Ivy Ruckman

1 Before the story even begins, the reader is presented with a news bulletin about missing hikers and a map of the Zion Narrows. How does this information affect the reader?

2 This book is written from more than one viewpoint. What are the strengths and weaknesses of changing the viewpoint character?

3 Throughout their ordeal, Clyde frequently thinks of something unpleasant that his father might do or say. What is the effect of having the survival action interrupted by these thoughts?

4 Ben and Clyde become emotionally attached to the tree that saved them from the flood waters. Have you ever been emotionally attached to an inanimate object? What do you think causes such attachments?

5 Audrey confesses that she and Steve aren't married, and that she has to stay where she can visit her husband in the hospital. Do you think that Steve will wait for Audrey and that the two of them will marry one day? Why or why not?

6 Rick gives an explanation of why he kept the granola bars a secret. Did Rick's explanation convince you?

7 Clyde indicates that words are one thing and actions are another. Do you think that when he recovers, Clyde will move with his mother to Eureka rather than wait to finish his senior year in school with his friends?

8 Gary stumbles into the party fairly late in the story. What particular strengths does he have that he offers to the group? Do you think the original group would have survived without Gary?

9 Amy has second thoughts and decides to cancel the wedding. Is there anything in the text to indicate to you that Rick is also having second thoughts?

10 Promises are made about keeping in touch with one another, but each member of the group will quickly be caught up in his or her own affairs again. Which members of the group do you think will really keep in touch? What makes you think that?

📖 Multidisciplinary Activities 📖

No Way Out
by Ivy Ruckman

1 Against the odds, the people in this story survived a flash flood. Flash floods are common in many parts of the country. Do some research on this topic. Where are such floods common? What causes them? Has there ever been a flash flood in your part of the country? Present an oral report to the class on what you have learned.

2 Neale succumbs to hypothermia. What is hypothermia? What causes it? How does it affect people? Find a doctor in your community who will come to your class and discuss hypothermia and what to do if someone gets it in the wilderness when medical assistance is not at hand. Arrange a convenient time for the doctor to visit. Prepare questions ahead of time. After the presentation, be sure to write a letter of thanks.

3 The author of this story had friends and neighbors who were actually caught in a flash flood. Such events usually make the national news. Unfortunately, dramatic accounts of hardship brought on by floods, hailstorms, winds, avalanches, blizzards, and the like are all too common. Search your own newspaper for an account of an event in which people's lives are put in peril by adverse weather conditions. Clip this story. Add to it whatever details you wish and create an original short story. Although you are writing fiction, use some of the information from the newspaper account. Share your story with the class.

 # *The Rain Catchers*

by Jean Thesman
Boston: Houghton Mifflin, 1991. 182p.

Type of Book:
This book is a realistic fantasy, written in the first person, present tense from the viewpoint of Grayling.

Setting:
In Grandmother's old house in Seattle and in San Francisco and San Diego.

Major Characters:
Grayling; her grandmother, Garnet; her aunt, Minette Minor; Grandmother's cousin, Olivia Thorpe; Minette's daughter, Yolande; Norah, Grayling's mother; Grayling's boyfriend, Aaron Ripley; Grayling's best friend, Colleen; Colleen's father, Dr. Clement; the doctor's new wife, Fawn; and Belle Russell, a friend who lives in Grandmother's house.

Other Books by the Author:
Appointment with a Stranger (Boston: Houghton Mifflin, 1989), *Cattail Moon* (Boston: Houghton Mifflin, 1994), and *When the Road Ends* (Boston: Houghton Mifflin, 1992).

—PLOT SUMMARY—

The story begins in summer, with Grayling and Colleen talking on the porch of Grayling's grandmother's house, waiting for teatime and for rain. Colleen and Grayling are planning to collect the first honeysuckle rain of summer for rinsing their hair tonight. Colleen hopes that it will rain before dinner. She has to go home for dinner tonight because her newest stepmother, Fawn, is expecting her.

Promptly at four o'clock, Grandmother Garnet prepares tea, and the girls listen to the women recite stories. Only Grayling's story seems unfinished. Grayling's father was run over and killed by a man who robbed a store. Then Grayling's mother Norah left Grayling with Grandmother and ran away.

Aaron Ripley is preparing Grandmother's house for painting. He enjoys the cookies and lemonade but keeps apart from the girls, through Grayling rather

likes him and wishes he would invite her out. The rains begin and the girls rush to put bottles out to catch honeysuckle rain where it drips off the roof. Later, they use the rain to rinse their hair.

Next Saturday, Grayling hears Belle carrying medicine to Olivia's room. Olivia is dying, and Grayling believes Olivia has extracted a promise from Belle to help her die. Norah, Grayling's mother, calls from San Francisco and suggests a visit to look at the schools there and consider moving out to live with her.

On the weekend, Grayling, Minette, Yolanda, and Colleen haul a bunch of junk out to the flea market north of Seattle. Colleen has brought a satin teddy that belongs to Fawn, her stepmother, and sells the teddy for 50 cents to a woman who knows Fawn and works out with her in the same gym. When they get home from the flea market, Grayling overhears her grandmother soothing Olivia by saying, "We promised you. It'll be any time you say."

When Yolande and Grayling pick Colleen up to go and visit her mother, Colleen tells them that Fawn's brother broke into a nunnery and is staying with them until his trial. Colleen's father has hired a lawyer, P. Q. Murphy, to represent him—the same lawyer who successfully defended the man who killed Grayling's father.

That Monday, Cornelius Ert arrives to do the gardening. Grayling is sent on a shopping trip. She suspects that she is being sent out of the house so that the older women can go ahead with their plan to help Olivia die. But when they get back home, Grayling finds Olivia still alive. Grayling takes Aaron his lunch, and he invites her to go out with him that night for pizza and a movie. She accepts. They talk and have a good time together. When they get home, Grayling is crushed to learn that Olivia is dead.

Grayling spies a wrecked hypodermic needle in the garbage pail and suspects that Belle has deliberately ended Olivia's life. Then she learns that when they let the dog Gip back into Olivia's room, the dog curled up on the pillow and also died.

The next day, Colleen shares with Grayling an unpleasant experience involving Fawn's brother Lance. Cornelius brings flowers in memory of Olivia and delivers a rose from Aaron for Grayling. Norah calls with arrangements for Grayling to fly out on a visit this Friday. The next day, Grayling and Aaron talk about the woods nearby and the statue there of two people kissing. Grayling returns to the house and Aaron to his painting. That afternoon, the family goes on a ferry and scatters the ashes of Olivia and Gip.

That night, Grayling goes out to the statue in the woods. Aaron joins her, which makes Grayling suspicious. She remembers that Belle wanted her out of the house the night that Olivia died, and, in fact, she finds out that Belle set up the date with Aaron. Grayling is upset, but she and Aaron exchange their first

kiss and walk home holding hands. Still, Grayling worries that because Belle had arranged the movie date, it was not real, and she thinks this kiss may not be real either.

Grayling flies to San Francisco and is met by her mother. They go to mother's house, walking up the steps on a hillclimb. Grayling remembers from her last visit that the hillclimb is lovely by day and terrifying by night. Her mother's house is like a fortress; all of the windows in the house are protected by ornamental grills, and she has a burglar alarm.

They take the trolley to lunch and stop at Norah's office. Norah is quickly sucked into the office routine, but Grayling gets tired waiting and says she'll go home. Instead of going home, however, Grayling buys postcards and a map, then goes to Fisherman's Wharf and gets lost.

She hears laughter and sees an enchanting young man who calls himself Dancer and offers her whatever she wants. Grayling asks directions to the Coit Tower knowing she can find her way home from there. Dancer flips open his coat and reveals watches and chains for sale. Then he becomes menacing, and Grayling flees, frightened. She does not tell her mother about the experience. That night, someone tries to break into the house next door. Mother grabs a gun and threatens the burglar, who races off. Grayling stares at her mother's gun but refuses to handle it.

On Saturday, Grayling and her mother shop. They stop at the office, and again Norah gets tied up with work. Grayling leaves and has lunch. Then she consults her map and goes back to the street where she had seen Dancer before. He approaches Grayling again, and she asks for a gun. When he asks how she will pay for it, Grayling dismisses him by saying if he had one, he would quote her a price. She walks away.

When Grayling gets home, she calls her grandmother. That night, Grayling asks her mother why she has been invited to move to San Francisco. Her mother says that Grayling is able to take care of herself now and that grandmother's house will not prepare her for the real world. They go out to dinner and a movie.

When they return home, Grayling hears someone at the window. Dancer has tracked her home and found her a gun. Grayling slams the door on him, saying she no longer wants it. She then tells the whole story to her mother, who arranges for them to leave in the morning on a trip to San Diego. She owns an apartment house there whose manager recently left. She wants to persuade one of the tenants to take on that job. Grayling is humiliated and wishes she had not been so stupid. Her mother says never to mention it again.

In San Diego, they go to the apartment house, which contains the apartment her parents had when Grayling was born. They visit the zoo and eat Chinese food in the apartment for dinner. The next day they visit Sea World and Old Town. As soon as Norah speaks to the tenant, they fly back to San Francisco.

Norah arranges for Grayling to fly back to Seattle the next evening, or earlier if she can get a cancellation, but Grayling wants to know why her mother left her. Reluctantly, her mother explains that the night before she left, she was in a store and saw the man who murdered Grayling's father. Norah drove away, and the man followed her. Norah finally turned off her car lights to get away. She abandoned the car in the woods and ran home to Grandmother's house. The reason the murderer was not convicted was because the lawyer persuaded everyone that Norah was drugged out of her mind and could not identify him. Norah could not get over the fact that the guilty man was never convicted. ·Feeling that she could never escape such men, she left.

Grayling fails to persuade her mother to come home with her to Grandmother. They go to the office, and from there Grayling goes to the airport. When Grayling arrives in Seattle, she is surprised to be met by Yolande, who explains that Colleen has argued with her father and moved to Grandmother's house.

When Grayling finally gets home, there is a happy reunion.

Grayling asks about the bruise on Colleen's face. Colleen explains that she took a bus to visit her mother last Sunday. Her father and Fawn went to the tennis club and left Lance at home. When Colleen returned home, she found Lance in her bedroom. He had pried open the lock on the desk and taken her money and gold bracelet. Lance tried to run away and knocked Colleen down when she tried to stop him. Colleen then called her father and insisted that he come home. Fawn stood up for her brother, and Colleen's father stamped out of the house, so Colleen came over to grandmother's. Grandmother has already called her lawyer.

The next morning, Grandmother takes Colleen into town, and when they get home they are both weary of lawyers and social workers. Then everyone goes down to the orchard to pick cherries. At 3:30 they head back to the house to prepare tea. Another honeysuckle rain comes.

Aaron helps Colleen and Grayling set out the jars to catch the rain water. He asks Grayling to go to a movie, but is interrupted when Dr. Clement drives up, intending to accuse Belle of doing wrong in connection with Olivia's death. Colleen lies and says that Grayling was alone with Aunt Olivia when she died, and was so upset by the death that she went away for a trip. Grayling backs her up. The women retreat into the house, leaving Dr. Clement out in the rain. Aaron comes inside to see if Grayling will go to the movies with him. The movie is poor, and they leave early, walk the mall, and have ice cream before returning home.

Dr. Clement finally agrees to let Colleen stay with Grandmother, and Grandmother agrees to renew Dr. Clement's lease. They hold a celebration dinner and invite Colleen's mother. Belle, who has been acting strangely, calls to say she will not be home for dinner. When Belle arrives later, it is with her suitor, a dentist, and she announces that she is planning to marry next week and to move to Hawaii. Before she leaves she suggests to Grandmother that Colleen and Grayling can fill the two chairs once filled by Olivia and Belle that are empty at tea time now.

Grayling and Colleen join the tea-time circle. One afternoon at the end of the summer, Grandmother gives her explanation of why she broke the hands off the clock. Life is too complicated if you worry about the minutes. She says that any kind of trouble, once contained, can be put to use. Grayling comments that it's the same with rain; honeysuckle rain can be used to give a fragrant rinse to hair. They have tea, and Grayling finally tells her story about meeting Dancer in San Francisco. Her story has a beginning, a middle, and an end, like all the stories shared at tea time.

📖 Discussion Starters 📖

The Rain Catchers
by Jean Thesman

1   This story is told in the present tense rather than in the past tense, the way most books are written. What effect is gained by writing in the present tense?

2   The clocks in Grandmother's house seem blind because all the hands have been snapped off. Grandmother eventually explains why she did this. Can you elaborate on Grandmother's explanation?

3   Tea time is a ritual in the book. Why are all the ceremonies surrounding tea time so important to the story?

4   The doll house in the story was never a doll house. It was a playhouse, a store room, and now a room used by a writer. Why does this particular building seems to be appropriate for Yolande?

5   Because Minette doesn't really need the money, why do you think she goes to the flea market every weekend?

6   Grayling finally forces her mother to explain why she left her with Grandmother as a baby. But the explanation is not very clear. In your own words, can you explain Norah's actions?

7   The Dancer is both menacing and attractive. Discuss the power that he seems to have over Grayling that causes her to return to him.

8   When Colleen sits at tea in Belle's chair, she seems to take on some of Belle's mannerisms. What traits do Belle and Colleen have in common?

9   Belle decides to marry and move away. If Olivia had not died in the way that she did, do you think Belle would have married and moved? Why or why not?

10   Near the beginning of the story and near the end, the young people put out bottles to catch the rain. Why do you suppose the author includes this scene twice?

From *The World's Regions and Weather.* © 1996. Teacher Ideas Press. (800) 237-6124.

📖 Multidisciplinary Activities 📖

The Rain Catchers
by Jean Thesman

1. Although it is disguised, the text of the story clearly indicates that Olivia made the other women in the house promise to help her die when she thought the time was right. Euthanasia, or assisted suicide, has been a topic of debate for many years. It often makes newspaper headlines. One doctor even earned the name of "Dr. Death" because of the number of times he helped terminally ill people end their lives. Many people remain adamantly opposed to euthanasia. With another interested person, make an oral presentation to your class showing both sides of this complex issue.

2. The characters in this story use honeysuckle rain as a final hair rinse. Hair products are a big item in the beauty business. What ingredients go into conditioners? Look at several leading brands. The prices will vary greatly. Do the ingredients vary? Perhaps you and your friends can try out three brands. Are some more effective than others? Report what you learn to the class.

3. San Francisco is a very interesting city. This story mentions trolley cars, Coit Tower, Fisherman's Wharf, and Golden Gate Park. These are just a few of the city's tourist spots. Write to the San Francisco Chamber of Commerce or check with a travel agent to secure pamphlets about the city. If you could visit the city for five days, what sights would you choose to see? Prepare five postcards to your teacher with a picture on one side and a paragraph on the back describing your favorite San Francisco sights.

♦ *Bridges* ♦

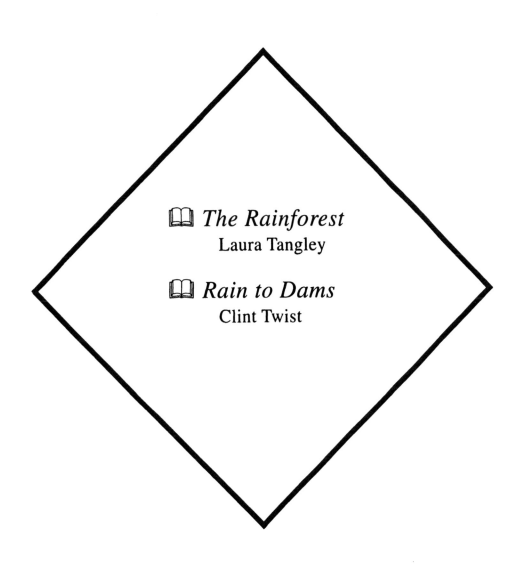

📖 *The Rainforest*
Laura Tangley

📖 *Rain to Dams*
Clint Twist

📖 *The Rainforest*

BRIDGES

by Laura Tangley
New York: Chelsea House, 1992. 136p.

This book is part of a series, Earth at Risk, designed to explore and promote awareness of critical environmental issues. Tropical rainforests are those that grow in a narrow band surrounding the equator; they represent less than 7 percent of the Earth's land area. Although they cover a small area, they provide the world's most diverse natural habitat.

Tropical forests once covered more than 4 billion acres. Now, more than half of these forests have disappeared, and another 51 million acres are lost each year. Most of these rainforests are being lost to commercial logging, agriculture, cattle ranching, and the development of dams, roads, and mines. Rainforest destruction is a complex problem, because poverty, hunger, and patterns of land distribution underlie the deforestation of these areas.

An enormous number of plants, insects, birds, and animals live in these forests. The tropical rainforests provide the world with about one-fifth of all the wood used in industry. Among the best-known tropical hardwoods are mahogany, teak, rosewood, and ebony. These woods are used for many purposes, including furniture, ships, bowls, and musical instruments. Forest products also supply us with rare medicines. The book concludes with ways individuals might help in slowing or preventing the loss of our world's rainforests.

Possible Topics for Further Investigation

1 Bats are strange creatures; although they fly, they are not birds. If you are interested in bats in general, you may become fascinated with the variety of bats that can live in a rainforest. Do some research on this topic. Check out magazines or books that have pictures of such bats. Photocopy some of these bat pictures, give them identifying captions, and prepare an informative classroom bulletin board on bats.

2 Many musical instruments are made from tropical hardwoods. See if you can arrange for a knowledgeable person from a music shop in your town, or someone who handcrafts musical instruments, to visit the class to show some instruments and discuss the woods from which they are made. What are the special qualities of tropical woods that make them so valuable for musical instruments?

3 A photograph in this book shows a banner in which the World Bank is being pressured not to fund development projects that damage rainforests. Yet the text also points out that because the problem is complex, a decision to boycott a country's tropical products can lead to economic problems that cause that area to accelerate rather than slow the deforestation of rainforests. Join with some classmates who are interested in the plight of the rainforests. Have each one select an area of concern to research. Then present, in the form of a panel discussion, the information that your group has learned.

 *Rain to Dams*

BRIDGES

by Clint Twist

New York: Gloucester Press, 1990. 32p.

This is a large format, easy-to-read book that is illustrated with colored drawings and photographs. It is part of a hands-on science series and is filled with simple projects that a student might perform using everyday items to demonstrate how water behaves.

The first section of the book discusses rain, clouds, and condensation, covering the rain cycle, artificial rain, and directions for making a rain gauge and carrying out an evaporation project. Cloud formations and fog are dealt with, and there is a simple project on condensation.

The middle section of the book explains solutions and solvents, freezing, thawing, and hailstones, and contains a discussion of floating and density (the ratio between the weight of an object and its volume). A section on surface tension is also provided. The section on water level discusses the water table and artesian wells and goes on to explain how people can raise water above the water table by the use of pumps and siphons. This is followed by information on water pressure and breaking through the surface of water.

The last portion of the books covers the ways in which dams are used to store rain water. Such topics as depths and pressure, hydroelectricity, water turbines, and generators are explained.

Possible Topics for Further Investigation

1   Page 19 of the book explains *meniscus*. If a container is not full of water, the meniscus will curve upward slightly at the sides in a concave shape. A full container will exhibit a convex meniscus. The text explains how to float a steel pin. Practice these experiments until you are successful with them. Then provide your class with a demonstration of what you learned about surface tension.

2   A liquid such as water exerts pressure in all directions. But water pressure increases with depth as the weight of water on top increases. This means that dams, which store enormous quantities of water, have to be designed to withstand pressure. You can demonstrate for your class the difference in pressure at various depths of water by using a large plastic soda pop bottle. Pages 26 and 27 of the text explain how you can puncture a bottle at various points, fill it with water, and observe the stream of water that comes through each puncture. The stream of water at the lowest depth will spray out the farthest from the bottle because it is under the greatest pressure.

3   Floating and sinking is particularly interesting to kindergarten students. At first they may guess that anything large, like a lemon or a tennis ball, will sink, and that anything small, like a paper clip, will float. Prepare a lesson on sinking and floating and present it to a kindergarten class. Do they gradually become more sophisticated in their guesses about what will sink or float as your lesson progresses?

Clouds, Rain, and Floods

■ Nonfiction Connections ■

📖 *Clouds*
Jenny Markert

📖 *Disastrous Floods and Tidal Waves*
Melvin Berger

📖 *Rain: Causes and Effects*
Philip Steele

📖 *The Sierra Club Book of Weatherwisdom*
Vicki McVey

📖 *Storm Alert: Understanding Weather Disasters*
Thomas G. Aylesworth

📖 *Weather*
John Farndon and Marion Dent

📖 *Clouds*

by Jenny Markert

Mankato, MN: Creative Education, 1992. 40p.

This is a large-format book with a limited amount of text. It contains many beautiful two-page color photographs.

The text explains how clouds are formed when cooling water vapor condenses into tiny droplets that float in the air and finally become thick enough to form a cloud. Once a cloud is formed, it constantly changes, thanks to air currents and rising and falling temperatures.

Because of the striking pictures, this is an exceptional book to help the student correctly identify three different types of clouds: stratus clouds, with a bottom edge usually less than 6,500 feet above the ground; billowy cumulus clouds; and wispy cirrus clouds that form at least four miles above the ground. In addition to the main classes of clouds, the book also discusses combinations such as stratocumulus, cirrocumulus, and cirrostratus clouds.

Although all clouds contain rain, not all clouds produce precipitation. Sometimes the water droplets simply continue to float in the air. Rain droplets form when tiny particles called ice nuclei (bits of salt, soil, or dust) float through the atmosphere and give the tiny droplets something to form around. There is mention of artificial cloud seeding that can take place where airplanes supply dry ice to serve as ice nuclei. Some water droplets never reach the ground. Others fall as rain, drizzle, sleet, or snow.

Possible Topics for Further Investigation

1 If you are an amateur photographer, you will no doubt be impressed by the beautiful color photographs of clouds in this book. Over a period of several weeks, shoot your own photographs of cloud formations. Keep a careful log of the date and time as well as the places where you shoot your pictures. Clip weather reports from your local newspaper for the same period. Put up a class bulletin board of your photographs. Try to name the various types of clouds in your pictures. Include the actual weather information. Did rain follow the appearance of certain types of clouds?

2 Some people enjoy looking at clouds and finding animals and other objects in their shapes. Write and illustrate a short picture book on changing cloud shapes. When it is finished, share your creation with an interested student or read it to a kindergarten or first grade class.

3 Cloud seeding has been the cause of several debates. Some people think we should learn more about it, seed clouds, and exert more influence over the weather. Others believe that seeding the clouds in one spot "steals" the rain from another spot where rain might have fallen if no one seeded the clouds. Have a friend join you in learning more about cloud seeding. Prepare a short debate on both sides of the issue to share with your classmates. After you debate, take a straw vote. Were most of your classmates persuaded that cloud seeding was a good or a bad idea?

📖 *Disastrous Floods and Tidal Waves*

by Melvin Berger
New York: Franklin Watts, 1981. 66p.

This book provides a good introduction to some of the disastrous floods that have occurred in various parts of the world. It is illustrated with black-and-white photographs.

The first section of the book, "Noah's Flood," details the activities of some explorers who searched for the biblical Ark near Mount Ararat. Although scientists do not agree on whether the biblical flood actually occurred, an English archeologist in 1929 found artifacts and a layer of mud and clay that date to about 4,000 B.C., showing that a sea had indeed covered the area.

In the sections devoted to river flooding, the book discusses the Nile and the Aswan High Dam built to try to control its waters, as well as the Hwang Ho, or Yellow River, in China, whose floods have killed more people than any other river in the world. The floods in the United States mentioned in this book include the 1972 flood of Rapid City, South Dakota; the 1889 flood of Johnstown, Pennsylvania; and Hurricane Agnes, which traveled up the Atlantic coast in June 1972, causing floods in Pennsylvania, Virginia, Maryland, Washington, D.C., New York, and New Jersey. Other sections of the book are devoted to seacoast flooding and include hurricane-caused floods such as the one that struck Galveston, Texas; tsunamis, such as the one from the quake in Prince William Sound, Alaska; and damage from collapsing dikes in Holland.

Possible Topics for Further Investigation

1. This book details several expeditions that investigated the story of Noah's Ark and the great flood mentioned in the Bible. Since 1981, several other explorations have taken place. Do some research on the great flood of the Bible. What are some of the important finds on Mount Ararat? In what years did these finds occur? Were the reports substantiated by photographs or other evidence? Give an oral report on what you learned from your research to the class.

2. The tsunami that resulted when a volcano on Krakatoa erupted caused the deaths of more than 36,000 people. The island itself fell beneath the sea. Later, a new volcanic cone pushed up out of the sea in the spot where Krakatoa had been. This new volcano was named the child of Krakatoa, or Arak Krakatoa. Such powerful forces of nature often give rise to legends and folktales. Write an original legend based on Krakatoa. You may illustrate it if you wish. Share it with your class.

3. Floods can be disastrous. The best defense is advance warning that allows people in the area to escape. Warnings often come from the National Weather Service. Find out more about this organization. When was it founded? What agency or agencies govern it? Where are National Weather Service offices located? What advances in information dissemination, computer programs, and weather prediction have occurred that have brought about major changes in the National Weather Service? Prepare a written report on what you have learned.

📖 *Rain: Causes and Effects*

NONFICTION CONNECTIONS

by Philip Steele
New York: Franklin Watts, 1991. 32p.

This is a large-format, easy-to-read book with photographs on almost every page. It is part of a series of books called Weather Watch.

The book begins with an explanation of the water cycle and includes an easy experiment to demonstrate evaporation. There are simple explanations of terms such as *drizzle, cloudburst, monsoons,* and *rainforests.* A world map is used to show the various rain belts. Five areas are depicted: those having under 4 inches of rain, 4 to 20 inches of rain, 20 to 39 inches of rain, 39 to 80 inches of rain, and more than 80 inches of rain. Photographs and drawings are used to depict certain types of clouds (cirrus, cumulo-nimbus, cumulus, nimbostratus, and cirrocumulus) and how the presence of certain clouds can be considered as indicators of rain to come.

An example of a weather map is used to show warm fronts, cold fronts, and occluded fronts. A satellite picture demonstrates the way that meteorologists follow the progress of clouds to help them in forecasting weather. There is mention of the importance of rain for both the irrigation of crops and to provide the right sort of habitat for various creatures. There is also a brief description of acid rain, its causes and effects. A glossary of terms is included.

Possible Topics for Further Investigation

1 This book explains in detail on page 16 how to make a rain gauge using a plastic soft drink bottle that has been calibrated with a felt-tip pen to mark a scale showing 5mm, 10mm, 15mm, etc. Make a rain gauge and use it to measure the rainfall in your area. Collect measurements for at least a month. Record your measurements and compare them with the information about rainfall given in a local newspaper. Do your readings match those announced in the paper? Share your information with the class.

2 Find a TV channel with a weather forecaster that you can watch each day over a period of two weeks. Also find a local newspaper that forecasts the weather, including expected highs and lows, showers, winds, rain, snow, etc., and clip this information for two weeks. Make graphs comparing the TV forecast with the actual weather and the newspaper forecast with the actual weather. Post these graphs on a bulletin board in your classroom. How accurate were the forecasts? Was one more accurate than the other?

3 On a map of the world, show the different rain belts. Include a legend that tells what the various colors mean in terms of annual inches of rain. Put this information up on a bulletin board in your classroom. Include a sheet of interesting tidbits. Among these might be the wettest place in the world, the driest place in the world, the maximum rainfall recorded for any one place in a 24-hour period, and so forth.

 *The Sierra Club Book of Weatherwisdom*

by Vicki McVey
Boston: Little, Brown, 1991. 104p.

 NONFICTION CONNECTIONS

This book can be used in any of the four weather sections discussed in this unit because it deals with many different kinds of climate. For our purposes here, however, the portions of the book dealing with rain will be emphasized. The book is illustrated with black-and-white sketches and provides detailed information for carrying out a number of weather-related projects.

In Chapter 5, a tropical rain forest right on the equator in Borneo is discussed. Borneo is almost completely covered with equatorial rain forest. Information is given about what it is like to live in this area, where rains fall almost every night.

Chapter 6 gives a detailed description of the hydrologic circle, which is a cycle that water goes through as it changes from ice to water to cloud and travels from the Earth's surface into the atmosphere and back down again. One molecule is traced from the Pacific Ocean into a cloud over Hawaii; on to Minnesota, where it falls as a raindrop; into the Mississippi; and back into the ocean through the Gulf of Mexico.

Frontal systems with cold and warm fronts are discussed in chapter 7. The low-pressure area that forms where fronts meet can result in snow or rain. The text explains that fronts move from west to east and, because cloud and precipitation patterns of warm fronts are different from those of cold fronts, forecasters are able to make weather predictions.

Possible Topics for Further Investigation

1 The excellent glossary of terms in this book might be of interest to you and your classmates as you study climate and weather. Make up a board game that can be played by two to six people. Use markers to travel through an interesting route. Include ways to quickly move forward or to fall back depending upon what space you land on due to the roll of a die. Devise any type of board that you wish. After rolling the die, before the player can advance, the player must draw the top card from a pile and satisfactorily define the word. For example, if the card *albedo* is drawn, the player must define it as "the amount of solar radiation reflected off a particular surface." Failure to successfully define the word means missing a turn. The words can be taken from the glossary and written on cards, with definitions on the backs of the cards.

2 Clear directions for making a rain gauge are given on pages 8 and 9 of the book. Make a rain gauge and mount it at home or school. Measure and record rainfall using your gauge. Compare it with local weather reports. How accurate are your readings?

3 For several weeks, keep track of the precipitation in five spots in the United States that are of interest to you. Choose one from the center of the country, two from the west, and two from the east. Make a chart to share your data with the class. List each city down the left side. List the dates across the bottom. In columns, list the amount and type of precipitation (rain/snow) for each city on each date.

📖 *Storm Alert:*
Understanding Weather Disasters

NONFICTION CONNECTIONS

by Thomas G. Aylesworth
New York: Julian Messner, 1980. 159p.

This book has only a few black-and-white photographs for illustrations. The text provides a good introduction to a number of factors about weather and might be used in any of the four sections of this unit of study. Emphasis here, however, will be on thunderstorms and floods.

The reader is informed that at any given moment there may be between two and three thousand thunderstorms going on. The conditions necessary for a thunderstorm are explained: a large surface area with warm moist air above it; little or no wind; rising air due to a cold front, mountains, or a very hot piece of land below the air; and the formation of cumulus clouds. Then the sun heats the ground, which in turn radiates energy back into the air, heating the underside of the clouds and causing the layer of air to expand. Pockets of warm air move up through the center of the clouds, which join to form cumulonimbus clouds. Water drops form but are held in the cloud by the updraft. These water drops eventually may become heavy enough to fall as rain or hail, creating a downdraft in the cloud. The downdraft causes a drop in temperature in the land below. This is usually followed by a downpour of rain or hail.

Chapter 10 points out that flooding can be caused by rain, melting snow, ocean surges, and such disasters as landslides and breaking dams. Several famous floods are discussed in detail, including the 1976 Big Thompson River Flood in Colorado.

Possible Topics for Further Investigation

1 Unfortunately, flooding is common throughout much of the United States. You have, no doubt, seen pictures in magazines, in newspapers, and on television of floods. Floods also are times of daring rescue, when people stranded and surrounded by water are saved through heroic efforts. Do some reading about some of the famous floods. Then write a fictitious newspaper account of a flood and a rescue. You may set the account wherever you wish, and it need not be true, but it should contain details that make your "reporting" sound authentic.

2 Understanding aspects of weather requires knowing something about wind. You might present the following experiment to show your classmates while explaining about winds. Draw a spiral on a sheet of paper. Then cut the spiral out and tie a thread through the center of your spiral. Hold the spiral on the thread so that it hangs above a lightbulb that is turned on and has had time to get hot. The spiral of paper begins to turn because hot air expands and rises.

3 Rain may make its way through creeks and rivers back to the ocean, where it will evaporate and eventually fall as rain again. Prepare a chart showing this water cycle. Include this experiment as part of your explanation. Put two cups of water into each of two tall, thin glass bottles. Put two cups of water into each of two shallow glass baking pans. Put one bottle and one pan in a warm spot and the other two in a cool spot. In three days, measure the amount of water in each container. Explain the differences.

 *Weather*

Edited by John Farndon and Marion Dent
London: Dorling Kindersley, 1991. 64p.

This large-format book is a part of a series called Eyewitness Guides. It is intended to serve as a "unique visual encyclopedia."

The book begins with a brief look at various aspects of the atmosphere and how people throughout history have tried to understand and predict the weather. It examines weather forecasting from old folklore to modern computerized techniques. The causes and effects of many different kinds of weather conditions, such as sunshine, clouds, cold, rain, wind, snow, fog, and thunder, are explained.

On many pages there are models that reveal the structure of clouds, fronts, and hurricanes in three dimensions. There are also many pictures of early weather forecasting instruments. Included are answers to many basic weather questions, such as "Why does it rain?" "How hot is a bolt of lightning?" "Why are clouds of different shapes?" "How can you recognize a warm front?" "What makes hurricanes occur?"

This book would be a useful resource for any of the four sections of *The World's Regions and Weather*. Because it is used here as a resource in "Clouds, Rain, and Floods," the sections of this book that are of special interest begin on page 24, "The Birth of a Cloud," and continue through the sections "A Cloudy Day," "A Rainy Day," "Fronts and Lows," "Thunder and Lightning," and "Monsoon."

Possible Topics for Further Investigation

1. It is still possible to get copies of *The Farmer's Almanac*, which uses natural signs to predict weather for the year ahead. Borrow a copy of this book prepared for the previous year. Compare the predictions with the actual recorded weather for a given period of time. Was the *Almanac* accurate? In what ways was it closest to being correct, and in what areas did it really miss in its predictions?" Share what you learn with your class.

2. You can construct a simple hygrometer to measure relative humidity. Take two pieces of wood approximately 6" wide by 10" long. Use one piece of wood for the base. Nail the short edge of the second piece of wood to the base so that it stands upright. Attach two Fahrenheit thermometers side by side on the upright piece of wood. Dip a strip of cloth, 1" wide by 10" long, into water. Wrap part of the strip of wet cloth around the bulb of one of the thermometers and tie it in place with a piece of thread. Let the rest of the strip dangle into a plastic glass beneath it. Fill the plastic glass with water so that the strip of cloth acts like a wick. If you fan the air in front of the two thermometers with a piece of cardboard, you will get lower readings on the wet-bulb thermometer. Why?

3. Bring a barometer into class. Record your readings three times a day. Also cut out and post the weather report from your local newspaper. Can you sufficiently correlate your barometer readings with the weather so that you can predict storms?

Part IV

Winds:
Hurricanes, Tornadoes,
and Typhoons

Hurricanes, Tornadoes, and Typhoons

● FICTION ●

📖 *Devil Storm*
Theresa Nelson

📖 *Night of the Twisters*
Ivy Ruckman

📖 *The Silent Storm*
Sherry Garland

📖 *Windcatcher*
Avi Wortis

◆ BRIDGES ◆

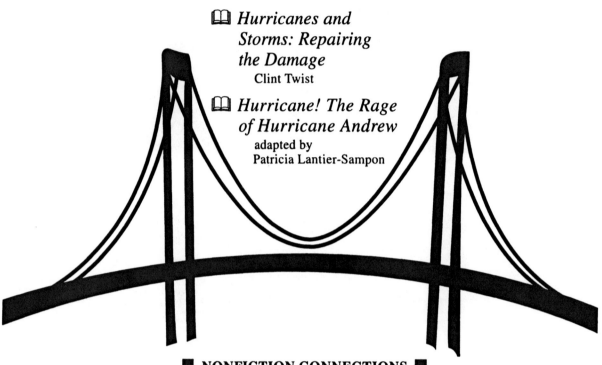

📖 *Hurricanes and
Storms: Repairing
the Damage*
Clint Twist

📖 *Hurricane! The Rage
of Hurricane Andrew*
adapted by
Patricia Lantier-Sampon

■ NONFICTION CONNECTIONS ■

📖 *Disastrous Hurricanes and
Tornadoes*
Max and Charlotte Alth

📖 *Hurricanes*
Sally Lee

📖 *Hurricanes and Tornadoes*
Norman Barrett

📖 *Storm Warning: Tornadoes
and Hurricanes*
Jonathan D. Kahl

📖 *Weather*
editors of *Science and Its Secrets*

📖 *Wind and Weather*
Barbara Taylor

—OTHER TOPICS TO EXPLORE—

—"Eye of the storm"	—Anemometers	—Sailing	—American Red Cross
—Erosion	—Wind chimes	—Waves	—Beaufort scale
—Windmill fields	—Chinooks	—Kites	—Civil Defence
—Air pollution	—Barometric pressure	—Weather balloons	

Hurricanes, Tornadoes, and Typhoons

● *Fiction* ●

📖 *Devil Storm*
Theresa Nelson

📖 *Night of the Twisters*
Ivy Ruckman

📖 *The Silent Storm*
Sherry Garland

📖 *Windcatcher*
Avi Wortis

 *Devil Storm*

by Theresa Nelson
New York: Orchard Books, 1987. 214p.

Type of Book:
This book is historical fiction, written in the third person from the viewpoint of Walter Carroll.

Setting:
The Bolivar Peninsula between the Gulf of Mexico and Galveston Bay.

Major Characters:
Walter Carroll, age 13; his father Richard; his mother Lillie, his sisters Alice and Emily; and an old tramp named Tom.

Other Books by the Author:
And One For All (New York: Orchard Books, 1989), *The Beggars' Ride* (New York: Orchard Books, 1992), and *The 25¢ Miracle: A Novel* (New York: Bradbury Press, 1986).

—PLOT SUMMARY—

The prologue is set in July 1900. An old Black man named Tom has come back to Bolivar. All sorts of strange tales about Tom circulate, both concerning his parentage, a possible treasure, and who he really is.

As Book 1 begins, 13-year-old Walter Carroll and his father Richard are loading watermelons into a wagon. Walter's father is proud of their crop and thinks that the melons will bring good money the next day in Galveston. In the distance is their house. Walter's sister Alice startles them when she sneaks up, carrying her little sister Emily. Before Alice goes back to the house, she teases Walter by saying that she has a secret.

The family gathers around the table, and after they eat, Walter's mother Lillie says that Alice found the remains of a campfire on the beach. Walter's father orders Alice not to go far from home alone.

Walter tumbles into bed shortly after dinner, but he is awakened in the middle of the night by Alice. She invites him to come down on the beach to see something.

He refuses, and Alice starts off without him. Then Walter gets up and follows her. They look at the moon reflected over and over again in the water. Alice and Walter run out into the magic "moonwater." Alice says that if they swallow some water, they will be able to read minds. Walter does not believe her, but they both swallow a little water when they are knocked over by a wave. As they run back to the house, they see a campfire down the beach.

The next morning, Walter milks the cow while Alice feeds the chickens. Crockett, their dog, is missing. Mr. Carroll hitches up the mule to take the melons into town. When they reach the boat that will take the melons to market, there is a crowd around Lester Barrett, who is telling stories. Walter and his father learn that the "crazy old colored tramp" has been seen. When Lester finishes his story, the men load their melons on the boat.

When they are on their way home again, the rain begins. Walter asks his father if they should worry about Tom.

112

His father says Tom has been around for a long time and tells Walter not to mention old Tom to anyone at home.

At noon, Walter's mother, Lillie, is nervous. Walter knows something has been wrong between his parents ever since his brother William died a year ago. Walter goes to the barn and thinks about Tom, who is supposed to be the son of Lafitte the pirate. Alice comes out and interrupts Walter's thoughts.

Walter tells Alice how he once saw Tom. Then he dreams of finding Lafitte's treasure and giving his mother a gorgeous necklace that will put away forever the black mourning ribbon she has worn around her neck ever since William died. The rain stops and Walter and Alice run down to the water to swim and play. Not far away, but out of sight, Tom sits scratching Crockett's ears and watches them.

The next day, Mr. Carroll has business in Galveston, and the children ride in the wagon with him to the train depot. Because of all the stories about a tramp being around, Walter has to stay home and look after the family. Mr. Carroll also suggests that they look for Crockett.

Mr. Carroll rides the train, thinking about how he misses the sea, but not sorry that he gave it up for his family. He wonders why Lillie married him. He knows that his wife blames him for the death of their child. If they had not been stuck in the middle of nowhere, perhaps a doctor could have reached them sooner and saved William.

A passenger on the train, Mrs. Sparks, sits down next to Mr. Carroll and asks if he has heard the news about old Tom. Mrs. Sparks tells him that yesterday the sheriff came looking for Lester Barrett and ended up making him a deputy on Bolivar because so many people were worried about old Tom.

When the children get home from the station, Walter finds his mother crying because it is the anniversary of William's death. He goes to work in the field. Alice runs up saying she has seen old Tom. She suggests they pack some food and visit him. They find Crockett with Tom and see Tom digging on the beach. While

Alice and Walter argue about whether to move closer, Old Tom calls them. Alice gives Tom the food she has brought from the kitchen, and Walter asks if Tom is looking for treasure. Toms says he has a sack of secrets. He lets Alice pull out a piece of driftwood. Walter looks at it closely and sees a face in the wood. Old Tom tells them a tale about the devil, a woman, a child, and a hurricane.

Walter hides the driftwood under his mattress. He works hard the next day, and his father returns from Galveston that evening. For the next three weeks, Walter and his father are busily clearing a field. Then it rains, and they cannot work.

Walter goes to the barn to milk the cow and finds Tom there. He goes back to the house and tells Alice to save some of her food for Tom. But during breakfast, Walter's parents notice the food Walter is saving in his napkin. Alice covers this by suggesting the food is for Crockett.

After breakfast, Alice and Walter pretend to take scraps to Crockett but actually take them to Tom. Tom lets Walter pull something out of the sack, and he comes up with a silver chain with a heart-shaped locket. Tom tells them a story about a girl who lived long ago and was captured by pirates. She and her baby survived a hurricane and then were sold to a white couple in New Orleans. When the child grew up, his mother gave him the locket and told him about his pirate father's treasure.

Alice cries over the sad story, and Walter says they cannot keep the locket. But Tom gives Alice a string of white shell beads that he says Indians used to wear. He tells them another story about an Indian graveyard before he leaves.

A week passes. Walter is working in the field with his father when Rupert Bland and Frank Buvens ride up, carrying shotguns. The two men say the old Black tramp is stealing chickens. Walter worries about Tom. Outside church, Walter hears some men plan to take Lester's vicious dog Samson and go hunting for Tom on Monday night.

Sunday night, Walter and Alice sneak out to warn Tom. They find him in the Indian graveyard and warn him. Instead of being frightened, he scolds them for being out at night and says that only the Gulf will ever be able to catch him.

As the children run home, Alice trips and hurts her ankle. When they come in sight of their house, they see that all the lights are on. Lillie is worried to death. Walter's father is furious with him and gives the boy a beating with a belt. After that, Walter sleeps 24 hours.

Tom is caught and taken to High Island. Walter goes wade-fishing and gets stung by a Portuguese man-o'-war. That night the pain keeps him awake. In a fever, he jumps up, pulls the driftwood and necklace from under his bed, and goes down on the beach and throws them into the Gulf.

The next chapter begins Book 2. Walter's fever has lasted for five days, but he recovers. Emily takes her first steps and delights everyone. That afternoon, Papa goes to Galveston again, leaving the rest of the family behind. He enjoys a meal with his relatives in Galveston, then waits to see a man at the bank. He reads a paper and checks the weather report, knowing his wife is afraid of storms. Although there is a storm off Florida, the report says that there is no weather for Texans to worry about.

Back at home, Lillie rocks the baby. It is stiflingly hot. On High Island, Tom is sitting in a small jail, thinking that the Gulf is coming for him tonight. He senses a storm on the way and worries about Walter and Alice. Lester drops in to visit and says that Tom will be released in the morning. Tom manages to convince Lester to let him go that night.

Alice wakes Walter in the morning, and they see the high waves. Walter goes out to milk the cow and finds Tom, who says they must leave because a terrible storm is coming, but Walter refuses to listen.

Mr. Carroll cannot get home because the barges are not working. He waits at the train station hoping that the waves will calm down by noon. At home, Walter suggests they should hitch up and drive to High Island. His mother refuses.

The wind gets stronger, and Tom hurries off to High Island. As he moves through the storm, he reflects on his wife and two children, who were sold away from him and then died of yellow fever. Then he thinks about Walter and Alice again.

Mr. Carroll can find no way to get home and frets. Back at his house, the water is up to the steps, and the wind is fierce. Lillie tries to keep cheerful but fails. The family hears someone at the door, but it is not Mr. Carroll. It is Tom. Tom says their only chance to survive is to make it to the lighthouse. Mrs. Carroll refuses to go, but Walter is finally convinced and insists that they leave. Lillie carries the baby, Walter carries Crockett, and Alice and Tom wade through the water toward the lighthouse.

Mr. Carroll has moved to the second floor of the train depot because of the high water. Wind is blowing the windows out of the building. He cheers up two little girls who are holding a canary in a cage and are waiting for their father.

Tom, Walter, Lillie, Alice, the baby, and Crockett struggle toward the lighthouse. The waves knock them over, but finally they see the light of the lighthouse. Back at the Union Passenger Station, where Mr. Carroll is, the roof blows off, but somehow the building stands. Gradually the wind slackens.

After the storm, Mr. Carroll finds a rowboat and oars and starts for home. When he gets close enough to land, he sees that his house is gone. He searches through the rubble but can find no trace of his family. Realizing that the water is too high for him to reach High Island, Mr. Carroll goes to the lighthouse.

Others have taken refuge in the lighthouse, including Mrs. Sparks, who had been on her way to Galveston. When the train stopped at Bolivar due to high seas, she and other train passengers came to the lighthouse. She is the one who spies Mr. Carroll approaching and rushes to tell the others. There is a happy family reunion, but Tom seems to disappear.

A rescuing party comes the next day to take the survivors to High Island. The Carroll family make plans to build a new house. Mama has changed and seems to love her husband again. They realize how fortunate they are when news of all the deaths reach them. Mr. Carroll's relatives have all been killed except for a pair of twins who were away visiting friends.

A busy year follows. A new house is built for the Carrolls and a new crop planted. Walter has had little time off, but on this occasion decides to walk to the beach. For the first time since the storm, Walter meets Tom on the beach. Walter asks Tom to come home with him, but Tom refuses. Before Tom goes, he gives Walter the little silver heart to give to Alice. In the spring, Tom's body is found near the Indian graveyard. He is by the grave of three people who died of yellow fever. The Carrolls bury Tom near William's grave.

📖 Discussion Starters 📖

Devil Storm
by Theresa Nelson

1 Book 1 begins with a quote from Ecclesiastes 3:15. Discuss what you think this particular verse of the Bible means. Why does the author include it here?

2 The Carrolls have given their pets the names of Texas heroes. If you were going to name a mule, a dog, and a rooster after local heroes, what name would you give each one and why?

3 Old Tom says, "Wondering is next door to wanting." What do you think he means by that?

4 When Walter goes to warn Tom that he's going to be hunted with guns and dogs, Tom scolds Walter. Walter feels shame and disappointment at this treatment. How would you feel?

5 Because Walter's father hates guns and has never said anything against Tom, why don't you think Walter told his father about his meetings with Tom and let his father give Tom warning?

6 Alice, though only nine, stands up to old Tom in the graveyard. Why do you think she speaks up like this even in such a frightening place?

7 What is the effect of having two white owls fly about and roost in the Indian graveyard?

8 After the storm, Bright Eyes, the canary, is so confused by the brightness of the moon shining through the roofless station building that the bird begins to sing. Why do you think the author included this detail?

9 A comic note throughout the story is the singing of well-meaning Mrs. Leola Sparks. What does this character contribute to the story?

10 The book concludes with an author's note and some acknowledgments that help the reader separate fact from fiction. Discuss whether or not you think the author's note should have been included.

📖 **Multidisciplinary Activities** 📖

Devil Storm
by Theresa Nelson

1 Hurricanes strike the coast of the southeastern United States every year. These hurricanes are given names. Do some research on this topic. When was the U.S. Weather Service founded? What sorts of weather predicting instruments do they rely upon? In what year did they begin to name hurricanes? What changes have been instituted in naming hurricanes? Is a name ever used more than once? What was the most destructive hurricane, in terms of lives lost, to ever strike the United States? When and where did that hurricane hit? Share the information that you learn about disastrous hurricanes with your class.

2 The Carroll family takes refuge from the storm in a lighthouse. Lighthouses in the United States have evolved over the past 200 years. The first lighthouses were built in New England to prevent shipwrecks. A Lighthouse Board was created by Congress in 1852. It was replaced in 1910 by the Bureau of Lighthouses. In 1939, the U.S. Coast Guard absorbed the Lighthouse Services. Research the history of lighthouses. Choose a lighthouse that is of interest to you and prepare a written report on its history. Include a picture of the lighthouse in your report.

3 In this story, the canary Bright Eyes and the rooster Sam Houston both survive the storm. Write an original short story set wherever you like. Be sure to include a storm and some sort of bird that survives the storm. Share your story with the class.

Night of the Twisters

by Ivy Ruckman

New York: Thomas Y. Crowell, 1984. 153p.

FICTION

Type of Book:
This is a realistic adventure story told in the first person from the viewpoint of Dan Hatch.

Setting:
Grand Island, Nebraska.

Major Characters:
Dan Hatch, a 12-year-old boy; his father; his mother; Dan's best friend, Arthur Darlington; Arthur's 14-year-old sister Stacey; Dan's Aunt Goldie; Dan's grandparents; and a neighbor, Mrs. Smiley.

Other Books by the Author:
In a Class by Herself (San Diego, CA: Harcourt Brace Jovanovich, 1983), *What's an Average Kid Like Me Doing Way up Here?* (New York: Delacorte Press, 1983), and *Who Invited the Undertaker?* (New York: Thomas Y. Crowell, 1989).

—PLOT SUMMARY—

This book begins with a one-page Associated Press bulletin dated June 4, 1980, describing the aftermath of a string of seven tornadoes that hit central Nebraska.

Dan Hatch starts the story by reflecting on red letter and black letter days. One of his red letter days was when he won a bike raffle. A black letter day was June 3 of last summer, which included something he had not expected—tornadoes.

The crafts class turned out not to be much fun. Dan's friend Arthur demonstrated the use of a bull-roarer, an Indian toy, and sheared off a lightbulb. The boys go swimming, but it turns cold, and everyone begins to leave the beach. As Dan and Arthur leave, Arthur's sisters Stacey and Ronnie Vae come running up. They want a ride on the boys' bikes to the Conoco station. Dan has a crush on Stacey and would be happy to give her a ride, but Arthur refuses to give Ronnie Vae a lift.

As soon as they walk in Dan's house, Dan's mother tells him to set the table. She looks tired. Baby Ryan is teething and just fell asleep. Dan invites Arthur to stay for dinner, and Arthur calls his mother. Then the baby wakes up.

The boys sit down to watch television. When Dan's dad gets home, he sends Dan to take care of his bike, which has been left out in the weather. As Ryan fusses and spits applesauce during dinner, Dan reflects on how much more pleasant their lives were six months ago before the baby was born.

Dan's father goes to Grandpa Hatch's farm to work on a tractor. Before he leaves, he makes a cutting remark to Dan. Dan and Arthur help by doing dishes and folding diapers. Dan's mother tries to put the baby asleep again. Aunt Goldie comes in just long enough to borrow a bowling ball.

Arthur and Dan go out to ride their bikes, but it is very windy. Dan suggests going to Arthur's, where he hopes to see Stacey. Arthur invites himself to spend the night with Dan. They start for Arthur's but stop first at Mrs. Smiley's. Arthur shows Dan her new storm door.

Things are chaotic as usual at Arthur's house. The two boys have a snack and return to Dan's house where they watch television. Dan's mother is in the kitchen sewing Grandma Hatch's birthday dress. Dan's mother calls Grandma Hatch, but no one answers the phone. Then an announcement comes over the television about funnel clouds and tornado warnings.

Dan's mother calls Aunt Goldie, but no one answers. No one answers at Mrs. Smiley's either, so Dan's mother drives over to check on her. Before going, Mrs. Hatch tells Dan and Arthur to take a flashlight and a blanket and put them in the downstairs bathroom. She tells them that if the siren sounds, they are to get Ryan and go downstairs. Mrs. Hatch leaves.

The siren sounds. Dan does not want to wake Ryan and listen to him cry. The siren stops, and the wind seems to die down. Arthur turns on the radio and hears "Tornado alert" just before the radio goes dead. On television are just the letters "CD" for Civil Defense Emergency. The lights in the house begin to flicker. Arthur suddenly wants to go home, but Dan forces him to go down to the basement.

Dan picks up Ryan and rushes to the basement. They crouch in the bathroom under a blanket. Above their heads, they hear furniture moving and windows popping. There is a crack, and the wall shudders; the house is being ripped apart. Chunks of the ceiling start to fall.

They all move into the shower stall under the blanket. For five or ten minutes, the twister seems to be right on top of them. The noise finally lets up. Then it begins to hail. Both boys worry about their families.

As the water keeps rising, the boys realize that the pipes are broken, so they leave the shower stall. When they emerge, they comprehend the enormity of the damage. Dan's house is gone; only the cement foundations and wreckage remain. The boys search for a way out of

the debris. They hear sirens. Then Stacey shouts to them. She tells them all of the Darlingtons have survived. She takes the baby, and the boys climb out. They run to Mrs. Smiley's house three blocks away, but there is so much debris, it is slow going. When they reach Miss Stevens's yard, they see Dan's mother's car, a battered wreck in a chain-link fence.

Dan digs in the wreckage of the car but can find no trace of his mother. He wants to keep digging, but his friends drag him off, saying she must have reached the neighbor's house. Suddenly, Dan sees his mother running toward him. She tells them Mrs. Smiley is safe but trapped in the basement of her house. They can see lights down the street, and they head toward them to find help.

The policemen and firemen have so much to do that they will not get to Mrs. Smiley's for some time. Dan's mother is persuaded to go with the baby to the shelter at Kmart while Stacey, Dan, and Arthur go back to Mrs. Smiley's house.

When they get back, Mrs. Smiley's house is still standing—it just does not have a roof. Dan, Stacey, and Arthur get inside, but the basement stairs are gone. Mrs. Smiley does not answer when they call. The boys manage to get down into the basement and finally find the woman, sound asleep on an old sofa. With some difficulty, they get her to climb up some old bedsprings and out the basement window. As they make their way down the street, they stop to talk with a fireman. He tells them that other tornadoes have touched down, including one around Phillips, which is near Grandma and Grandpa Hatch's farm.

The fireman tells them to leave the area as quickly as possible because of the danger of fires and explosions. They go back to the corner and wait for a minibus. The seats fill up before they get on, but a young man gives his seat to Mrs. Smiley, so she leaves while Stacey, Dan, and Arthur wait.

Two police cars take those who could not fit into the minibus. An officer named Kelly starts for Kmart with Stacey, Dan, and Arthur. There is a lot of static on the radio, but they hear something about

"Meves Bowl" and people trapped. Dan knows that Meves Bowl is where his Aunt Goldie was headed when she picked up the bowling ball earlier.

Suddenly the patrol car turns around as a new tornado strikes them. The windshield breaks, and although Officer Kelly is accelerating, the car does not move forward. Finally the car heads forward. Officer Kelly has glass in his eyes and cannot see, so Dan moves up and drives the car to the police station. They make it to the Public Safety Center, where the officer immediately receives help. Dan, Arthur, and Stacey go upstairs in wait in the women's section of the jail. Other people there describe the disasters they have been through.

As they sit in the jail, Stacey tells the others that her mother is pregnant; Arthur worries that he might have caused the tornado by playing with the bull-roarer; and Dan wonders if he caused it by wishing Ryan was not around. The water goes off; then the auxiliary power fails, and the lights go off in the jail.

Early the next morning, they hear National Guard helicopters overhead. They try to phone Dan's grandmother and the armory where Arthur's family is, but the lines are down. A policewoman offers to try to drive them to their parents. They go to the armory first and find Mr. Darlington. Then Mrs. Minetti tries to drive Dan to Kmart but cannot get through. She parks, and Dan goes forward on foot.

When Dan gets to Kmart, he learns that all the civilians have been evacuated and scattered at facilities across the town. Dan decides to go through the park and try to get home, knowing his family will come there. Then he hears the sound of a pickup truck. It is his dad with the rest of the family. Dan learns that the tornado near Phillips missed the farm, and that Dan's father found Dan's mother and Ryan at the Presbyterian Church.

They drive to where their house once stood and survey the wreckage. Dan's father says that they'll all be living on the farm for a while.

During the next year, Dan's family stays at his grandparents' farm, and Arthur stays with them. The large Darlington family is split up for a while. Thanks to insurance and government loans, most families are able to stay and rebuild their homes on the old foundations. Many people and organizations pitch in to help. Mrs. Smiley serves food to anyone who needs it in her yard. Eventually, many families, including Dan's and Arthur's, are given government-issue trailers to live in while their new homes are being built.

When the story ends, it is a year later, and families are gathering to celebrate the anniversary of their survival. One of the few who misses the anniversary is Mrs. Smiley, who died during the year. The Darlingtons come, and the thanksgiving feast at the Hatch's is about to begin.

📖 Discussion Starters 📖

Night of the Twisters
by Ivy Ruckman

1 Dan is very hurt by the remark his father makes just before leaving for Grandpa's farm. Why did he make that remark?

2 What effect is created by having Mrs. Darlington give all her children rather exotic names taken from current romance novels?

3 Mrs. Smiley has replaced her ancient patched screen door with a new storm door. What significance does this have in the story?

4 When Dan discovers his mother's mangled car, his friends have to tear him away from it because he is certain his mother is caught beneath it, while they believe she is at a friend's house. Do you think it was realistic to have Dan continue to want to dig in the car rather than leave and search for his mother?

5 Dan remembers that he wanted to leave Ryan asleep in his crib when the storm started so he wouldn't have to listen to him cry. After the tornado hits, Dan is grateful that he saved Ryan and promises to be a great big brother. Do you think living through the storm has changed the relationship of these two brothers?

6 In frightening times, people sometimes make jokes. In this story, one of the ladies laughs about having to cancel the church bazaar. Have you been in a frightening fix where someone found something funny in the situation? What was it?

7 Although he doesn't really mean it, Grandpa Hatch talks about selling the farm and moving to Arizona. If you had lived through this storm, would you want to rebuild or move? Why?

8 Because the water is contaminated, the survivors couldn't drink water for a long time. If you had to go for weeks without water, what would you choose to drink instead?

9 One loose end in the story was Police Officer Kelly. Would you have liked to learn about what happened to him, or did you think he was not an important figure in the story?

10 If you had written the story, would you have had Mrs. Smiley die before the anniversary celebration? Why or why not?

📖 **Multidisciplinary Activities** 📖

Night of the Twisters
by Ivy Ruckman

1. Although the tornado itself is frightening and the aftermath fearful, there are some very funny scenes in this story. One of these is the way in which Stacey, Dan, and Arthur manage to get 81-year-old Mrs. Smiley out of her basement. Study this section of the book, then illustrate this scene. You may use any medium that you wish, but be sure to include all four of these characters from the story. Share your art work with the class.

2. The American Red Cross has been around for a long time and is famous for its help after all sorts of disasters. Find out more about this organization. Who founded it? How many chapters are there across the country? How is it supported? Is there a Red Cross office near you? How is the Red Cross alerted and organized to assist in a disaster? Through research, which if possible should include talking with some Red Cross members, find out what you can and share your information with your class.

3. Do some research about tornadoes and share what you learn by using colors and flags on a map of the United States that you put up on a class bulletin board. In the United States, where are tornadoes most common? In terms of loss of human life, when and where did the worst tornado hit? In terms of property loss, when and where did the worst tornado hit? What is the closest that a tornado has come to your town?

 *The Silent Storm*

FICTION

by Sherry Garland
New York, NY: Harcourt Brace Jovanovich, 1993. 240p.

Type of Book:
This is an adventure/survival story told in the third person from the point of view of 13-year-old Alyssa.

Setting:
Near Galveston Island.

Major Characters:
Alyssa, a 13-year-old girl; her grandfather, Bruce MacAllister, known as Captain Mac; Alyssa's Uncle D; Alyssa's brother Dylan; Alyssa's Aunt Melinda and Uncle Steven and their daughter Cecile; and a 15-year-old boy, Ty DuVal.

Other Books by the Author:
Best Horse On the Force (New York: Henry Holt, 1991), *Shadow of the Dragon* (San Diego, CA: Harcourt Brace Jovanovich, 1993), and *Song of the Buffalo Boy* (San Diego, CA: Harcourt Brace Jovanovich, 1992).

—PLOT SUMMARY—

The prologue, called "The Devil Wind," reveals that Alyssa loved to hear stories of storms and the sea from the sailors in her family, Uncle D and her grandfather, Captain Mac. Alyssa hoped for a great "Devil Storm," in her lifetime. Then she got her wish.

Chapter 1 begins on Alyssa's thirteenth birthday. She has gone riding early in the morning on her horse, Stormy. Near a cove, she hears three boys talking and watches them unobserved. She realizes that they are about to take her green boat. She wants to scream at them but cannot, for she has not spoken since her parents drowned three years ago.

Two of the boys, Ty and Ernie, send Hal to get their fishing gear, and they prepare to go out in Alyssa's boat. Alyssa gets closer to the two boys and hears them talking about Hurricane Berta. Then Hal calls the boys to come and see what he has found.

When Ty and Ernie join Hal, Alyssa gets in her boat and pushes off. The boys have found Stormy, but Alyssa thinks the horse can take care of itself. She gets away, but the boys shout that Alyssa had better bring the boat back, because they have her horse. Alyssa brings the boat back in. She fights with the boys and rescues both Stormy and her boat. Ty admires this girl who fights so hard. He makes the best of the situation by waving and calling "Bye, bye, Blondie."

As Alyssa heads home, she reflects that things are not going well at school. She agrees with the doctors that if she could remember exactly what happened the day that the boat sank and her parents drowned, she might be able to speak again. She misses her mother, but at least she knows her mother is in a grave marked with a white stone angel. Her father's body was never found.

Alyssa puts Stormy in his stall near her grandfather's house, then feeds the

123

horses and cleans out the stalls while listening to the radio. She marks the position of the approaching hurricane with a red pin on the tracking charts she keeps tacked to the wall. Then she hears Uncle D drive up and sees him go into the house to talk with grandfather, who is depressed and wants to sell the horses and move back to Scotland to be buried. He says that if he does move to Scotland, he will leave Alyssa with her Aunt Melinda.

Aunt Melinda took in Alyssa and her brother Dylan three years ago, right after the accident. Alyssa hated it there. The house was like a museum, because Aunt Melinda's young son Charlie had died, and his room was kept like a shrine. Alyssa did not want to stay at any house that was not near the sea, because she hoped that one day her father would walk up the beach to her.

Captain Mac tells Alyssa to clean up because her aunt, uncle, brother, and cousin are coming. Alyssa goes to her room and tries to write a note to Captain Mac asking him not to go away and send her to live with Aunt Melinda. Then Alyssa rips up the note, runs outside, and rides off on Stormy.

Alyssa sits on an dead tree trunk and looks out to sea. Ty DuVal comes up the beach and explains to Alyssa that he only intended to borrow her boat for a couple of hours. He has a sprained ankle, so Alyssa manages to convey to him the idea that she will give him a ride on Stormy. Because Ty feels bad that he has caught no fish, Alyssa shows him where to catch some big ones. They agree to meet in the morning and go fishing.

When Alyssa gets home, her relatives are there. They are all dressed up, while Alyssa looks a mess, carrying a flounder she caught. Dylan begins to gasp, and Aunt Melinda acts as if he's allergic to fish. She calls the way Alyssa looks disgraceful. Uncle Steven tries to get Dylan to look at the fish and even suggests going fishing. A scene ensues, and Alyssa ends up throwing the flounder at her cousin Cecile.

Later, Alyssa puts on a frilly dress to go out to lunch, but this does not suit Aunt Melinda, who says they'll shop for clothes on the way to the restaurant. They buy a frilly blue jumpsuit for Alyssa and then go to lunch. When they take Alyssa home, Aunt Melinda and Uncle Steven explain that they will be staying the night in their beach house but will come by in the morning to pick Alyssa up and take her to live with them.

The next morning, Alyssa packs her duffel bag with clothes, having decided to run away. She writes a note and checks on her grandfather before she goes out to the stables. When Alyssa goes to the kitchen, she finds a chocolate cake with 13 candles that Captain Mac made for her. There is also a present: an heirloom locket with pictures of her mother and father inside. Alyssa puts on the locket and eats a piece of cake, then goes to the stables. She turns on the radio for news of the storm before saddling Stormy and taking her skiff back to the bayou to tie it to a cottonwood tree.

Then Alyssa sees Ty, who wants to go fishing. She does not think this is a good idea with the storm on the way, but she does not want to disappoint him, so she help him catch a flounder. Then she writes Ty a note telling him she's running away. Ty suggests that she come to his shrimp boat. They can take Stormy home, and he will give her a ride on his bike to the boat. But when they get to Captain Mac's, Alyssa's relatives are already there.

Ty tells everyone he is Alyssa's fishing buddy. He takes Dylan for a bike ride. Cecile rides around the corral, then races her horse down the beach. The horse leaps a fence, and Cecile falls off. When Aunt Melinda and Uncle Steven return, there is another row. Alyssa hides until her relatives leave to take Cecile to the doctor's office. Dylan stays behind to ride on Ty's bike, but Ty says he has to go home and mend shrimp nets. When Dylan asks to see Ty's boat, they take an old bike in the garage that is just big enough for Dylan.

As Ty, Dylan, and Alyssa leave, it starts to rain. They get to the shrimp boat and meet Ty's mother and his two sisters, Suzanne and Marie. The children play a game of Monopoly, and an hour quickly passes. Suddenly the boat motor starts. Ty's stepfather Randon has come home. Alyssa knows that she and Dylan should go home, or Aunt Melinda will be frantic. Randon is in a bad mood and punches both his wife and son. Ty tells the others to stay quietly below. The boat heads toward the deep waters of Galveston Channel.

As Alyssa sits below deck, memories of three years ago and the boat accident that claimed her parents begin to surface. She remembers that she had hid in her parents' boat the day it sank. Her father had gone out to help rescue some tourists in a yacht. She was supposed to stay behind, but she hid in the boat because she wanted to see the rescue.

Randon hears someone coughing below deck and discovers Dylan and Alyssa. The two go up on deck and are joined by Ty, who does a little trawling. Alyssa bails bilge water from the engine room. An hour later, Randon hauls the nets in and tells Ty to take care of the catch while he takes a nap.

They come upon a boatload of Vietnamese fishermen who need a fuel line. Ty wants to help, but Randon wakes up and refuses to give aid. Randon beats Ty and threatens to toss Dylan to the sharks, so Alyssa throws a bucket of bilge water in Randon's face. Randon knocks Alyssa down. Ty's mother comes up behind Randon and hits him over the head with a shovel.

They carry Randon inside the cabin, and Ty heads the boat back to Galveston. When they pass the Vietnamese again, Ty tosses them a piece of fuel line. The storm worsens and, though everyone bails madly, the boat rolls to one side, the engine room fills with water, and the engine stops.

Ty radios a Mayday signal. Then they get into a raft and begin paddling toward shore. They do not get far before they encounter the Vietnamese boat. The Vietnamese haul them aboard and maneuver toward Galveston Island. Alyssa wants to get off the boat now. She thinks she and Dylan can make it to grandfather's before the next surge of the storm hits.

Leaving the others in the boat, Dylan, Ty, and Alyssa climb into a raft and row to shore, but they are 10 miles from Captain Mac's. They hitch a ride with some men in a telephone repair truck, who drive them most of the way home until the road becomes impassable.

The children walk to Uncle D's cafe. The building looks sturdy enough to protect them, and Ty wants to stay there, but Alyssa feels she has to get back to her grandfather's and make sure that the horses are safe.

When they get to Captain Mac's, no one is there. The horses are gone too. Alyssa thinks that her grandfather and Uncle D are holed up on high ground in an old shelter in an abandoned cow pasture. The three children fight their way through the storm to the shelter. Uncle D is there, but Captain Mac has left in Uncle D's jeep to look for Alyssa. Alyssa and Ty leave Dylan at the shelter and start down the jeep road on Stormy. They find the jeep, which has overturned; Captain Mac is injured. Alyssa and Ty right the jeep and, with Stormy's help, get out of the muddy ditch and drive Captain Mac to the shelter. They wait in the shelter until the eye of the storm is over them and things calm down. Then Uncle D, Ty, Dylan, and Alyssa try to get Captain Mac to the hospital in the jeep.

They make it to a hospital. Captain Mac is in serious condition and keeps mumbling about Alyssa. The doctor says it will help if Alyssa can reassure him that she is all right. Alyssa tries to speak but cannot. She runs from her grandfather's room out to the breezeway. As she stands there, she remembers the boating accident. Her father put her in a lifeboat and went back to help her mother, who was tangled in ropes. Before she left, her father told her to hush her crying and pleading and to be brave. Alyssa promised not to say another word until her father came back.

Alyssa understands now why she has not spoken and accepts the fact that her father is dead. She goes back into the hospital and talks to her grandfather. He rallies. Uncle D and the children stay at a Red Cross Shelter that night, and early the next morning, Uncle D phones Uncle Steven and Aunt Melinda, who hurry over. Aunt Melinda frets about Dylan, but Dylan insists he's fine and accuses Aunt Melinda of hating him. Alyssa knows that her aunt is overprotective because of losing Charlie, so she talks to Dylan, and he apologizes to his aunt.

Uncle D, Ty, Alyssa, and Dylan check on the cafe and find it still standing. And, although they are wet inside and out and have lost part of the roof, Captain Mac's house and stables have survived too. There is a lot of cleaning up to do, and Ty offers to help. Alyssa thinks that with paint and advertising, their business might pick up again. Then they go to get the horses. Ty stays while Alyssa takes Dylan to the spot where she left her skiff and tells him about his mother and father. She explains to him why she did not speak for so long, and although she is not sure where they will live now or what they will do, they will be together.

📖 Discussion Starters 📖

The Silent Storm
by Sherry Garland

1   What special effects does the author gain by starting the story on the morning of Alyssa's thirteenth birthday?

2   Alyssa knows she is not doing well in school. What sorts of questions would she score high on if they were on her exams?

3   Holly called Alyssa twice after her parents were drowned and invited Alyssa to her birthday party. Then she gave up on her friend. What more might Holly have done? Do you think this would have made a difference in Alyssa's life? Why or why not?

4   When Dylan comes to visit, Alyssa can hardly recognize him. He is pale and nervous, bites his nails, is afraid of fish, etc. What has caused him to change so much?

5   Even though three years have passed, Alyssa continues to believe her father did not drown at sea. Why does Alyssa continue to hope that her father is alive?

6   When Randon starts the boat motor, Alyssa stays below deck. If she had gone up, what would have happened? Do you think that Randon would have put Alyssa and Dylan ashore, or do you think he would have struck them as he did his own son and wife?

7   When they are rescued, Randon behaves well in the Vietnamese boat. Do you think he has permanently changed for the better?

8   Alyssa's father had to break his promise, and Alyssa broke her promise. What other kinds of situations might cause promises to be broken?

9   Where do you think Alyssa and Dylan will live after Captain Mac gets out of the hospital?

10   Do you think that Ty and Alyssa will continue to be friends? Why or why not?

📖 Multidisciplinary Activities 📖

The Silent Storm
by Sherry Garland

1 Alyssa knows a great deal about "Urican," what the Indians call the devil wind. They say it is more than whirling wind and water; it is a living creature with a will of its own. Using chalk or another medium of your choice, make a picture of "Urican." How will you represent two things in your picture: the hurricane itself and the creature behind the wind? Share your art work with your class.

2 Although this book is fiction, the author became fascinated with hurricanes when she was the librarian for the oceanography and meteorology departments at Texas A&M University. She based the book on her experiences with Hurricane Alicia in 1983. Do some research. Find out more about Hurricane Alicia. How much damage did it cause? Were lives lost? What cities and states did it strike? Write a report on what you learn and share it with the class. Cite your references.

3 Throughout the story there is discussion of what is legal and what is not legal for the shrimp fisherman. There are times when certain types of nets and baits can be used. For a food fish in which you are interested, find out the regulations that govern its catch. Where is this fish abundant? What are the times when people can fish for it? Is this a major source of food for the world? How many tons of this fish are caught annually? What are the penalties for disobeying the regulations that pertain to catching this fish? Report what you learn to your class.

 *Windcatcher*

by Avi Wortis

Bradbury Press, New York, NY 1991. 124p.

Type of Book:
This is a realistic adventure story, told (for the most part) in the third person from the viewpoint of Tony Souza.

Setting:
Off the Connecticut shore.

Major Characters:
Tony Souza, an 11-year-old; his Grandmother; and Chris Carluci, a young woman who teaches Tony to sail.

Other Books by the Author:
Blue Heron (New York: Bradbury, 1992), *Encounter at Easton* (New York: Pantheon Books, 1980), and *The Man Who Was Poe* (New York: Orchard Books, 1989).

—PLOT SUMMARY—

The book begins with an account of a shipwreck in 1777. Mr. Littlejohn, sailing on the *Swallow*, is awakened in the middle of a storm. At first he is concerned about saving a treasure chest that contains the payroll for General Burgoyne's royal army in the north. Later, he only worries about saving his life.

The main story of the book begins in chapter 1. Tony Souza is just beginning his summer vacation and wants to use the money he has saved from his paper route to buy a motor scooter. Because Tony is only 11, his father reminds him that even if he bought a scooter, he would not be allowed on the road with a motor vehicle until he was 15.

Tony goes off to find what he might buy instead of a motor scooter and sees a small boat, a *Snark*, on sale. As he is going to spend three weeks of his vacation at his Portuguese grandmother's house on the Connecticut shore, the boat seems perfect. After some checking, his parents agree that he can buy the boat if he obeys certain conditions.

Tony goes to Swallows Bay with his new boat. The western side of the bay is called Joshua Point, the eastern side Hycock Point, and between the two is Swallows Bay Harbor. A statue at the harbor honors Captain Ezra Littlejohn, 1731–1821, the founder of the town.

Grandmother Souza greets Tony and his father, and they go into her house. Up in the bedroom that Tony will use is a three-masted British sailing ship in a bottle. Grandmother took this boat out of storage in honor of Tony's interest in sailing. The model is called *Swallow*.

Tony takes his first sailing lesson from Chris Carluci, an experienced sailor whose family owns a fish shop. As he reaches the dock, Tony sees two people racing off in a speed boat. Chris says they are looking for treasure. During his lesson, Tony manages to capsize the boat in shallow water. Overall, however, he does well. In a bicentennial edition of the town newspaper, Tony reads a little information about Swallows Bay. There are many stories of buried treasure in the area, but no proof has been found.

Tony's grandmother teaches him a few words of Portuguese, including *marinheiro*, sailor, and *barco a vela*, sailboat. In the morning, he looks at the statue by the harbor again and notices that the spyglass in the captain's hand is a real one. Chris watches the two treasure hunters go out on the water again.

After Tony's father leaves, Grandmother Souza drives Tony to get clams at the far end of Joshua Cove at a marshy tidal flat. She eats one of the clams raw, but Tony says he will wait until they are cooked.

When Chris takes Tony out for his second sailing lesson, she puts a plastic bottle aboard to serve as a bailing scoop for the boat. Tony does even better at sailing this time. After an hour's practice in Joshua Cove, they head toward Sachem Head. From a distance, Tony sees the Thimble Islands. Chris explains that there are crazy currents out there and that landmarks there change overnight when a big hurricane hits.

After a clam chowder dinner, Grandmother suggests that Tony might want to look for treasure while he visits. She thinks that to succeed they need to know more about Captain Littlejohn.

The next day, Tony's sailing lesson is moved from afternoon to morning because it looks as if a storm might be coming. In fact, the storm hits while Tony and Chris are sailing, and Tony capsizes the boat again. But they quickly right it and head in. Chris's brother tells Tony that even if anyone does find a treasure, it will belong to the state of Connecticut because of the laws about salvaging treasure. Grandmother takes Tony to the Guilford Library to learn more about the treasure. Both read things and compare notes about Captain Littlejohn.

The next day, Tony goes out sailing alone, but his Grandmother makes him promise to stay close to shore and to come by the dock in an hour so she can check on him. Tony does this and then goes out sailing again. He sees the motorboat aim for the Thimble Islands, and he heads there too. Before long, he gets lost. As he

tries to find his way back, he comes upon the motorboat. The man on the boat, which flies a white flag with a red slash, waves him away, saying they are diving. Although the man will not give Tony directions, the boy eventually finds his way home. His grandmother was worried because he was gone longer that he was supposed to be, but she says she will get him a compass and a watch. Tony studies a map trying to figure out where he actually was that day and where the treasure seekers were diving.

When Tony and his grandmother go to buy the watch and compass, they see in an antique shop a ship in a bottle that is much like theirs. Later, Tony takes Grandmother out in his boat, and while they are sailing, the motorboat comes in, and the couple stare at Tony. He drops his grandmother off and goes sailing again for another hour. When the couple from the motorboat go on land, Tony peers into their boat and sees that their diving equipment has never been used. Then, noticing that the two are watching him through binoculars, he sails off, but is soon chased by the motorboat, which deliberately swamps his boat. Tony rights his boat and heads back to land.

That night he studies his library book and notices the entry about the sinking of the *Swallow* in 1777, and also that one of the Thimble Islands is called Money Island. He shares his information with Grandmother. The next day, the two go back to the antique shop with their model ship. The dealer offers to buy their ship, saying that it is probably an 1810 model and worth $200 to $400. The name of the carver is probably somewhere in the cabin, but he is not able to see it.

Grandmother invites Chris over for lunch to tell her about what happened between the motorboat and Tony. Chris gives Tony another sailing lesson, but she does not have time to go treasure hunting with him. At night, when his grandmother is asleep, Tony pries open the model boat. He finds a lens inside, fastened in place with wax. He can also see some letters that are too tiny to read. Under a bright light and using the little lens, he reads, "Ezra Littlejohn, Quartermaster."

The next day, Tony wants to go sailing, despite the threat of rain and fog. He promises his grandmother not to hunt for treasure and that he will be home by one. Remembering that Littlejohn designed his own statue, Tony looks it over again. He cleans the spyglass and sees that the big lens is still in place. Then he tries fitting the small lens from his ship model into the small end of the statue's spyglass. It fits. Looking through the spyglass, he sees three islands in the Thimble Islands group. After checking the old map in his grandmother's house, Tony tentatively identifies them as Stooping Bush, Hogshead, and Money.

Tony notices a shift in the wind but continues sailing anyway and goes into the Thimble Islands. He gets lost again, but this time he has his compass with him. Again he sees the couple from the motorboat and makes a plan to approach them from a direction where they cannot see him so he can spy on them. Finding it hard to spy from his fast-moving boat, he goes to Hogshead Island, strips off his orange life jacket, and decides to stay there just a short time to look. He waits until both people are in the water and then walks over to get the number off their boat.

While Tony is in close, the man who is diving comes up and sees him. The man yells at him, and Tony runs back to where he left his own boat, but the *Snark* has drifted off. Tony hides and watches the motorboat go away. Then he decides to try to return to the mainland by swimming from island to island.

First he swims toward Money Island, but the currents are so strong that he is exhausted when he finally gets close to land, and he is not even sure which island it is. He drops one of the sneakers that he tied to his belt loop, and he dives to retrieve it. While diving, he sees some objects, possibly bones. Then he wades ashore on the rocky island and falls asleep, exhausted.

When Tony awakes, it is gray and dim. His watch has stopped, and he has lost his compass. He walks around the island and sees another island not too far away in the fog, but he cannot make it out clearly. Hungry, he eats some raw clams. Continuing to walk, he comes upon the Snark. Debating whether to stay until morning or try to sail home, lost and in the dark, Tony decides to sail, because he knows his grandmother will be worried. While in the fog, he thinks about the bones that he saw while diving for his sneaker and realizes they may mark the site of a shipwreck.

Then Tony sees stars and eventually a light. He shouts to the light, thinking someone is looking for him. But the boat that comes toward him is the motorboat with the couple that he fears. They question him about what he has seen, and he lets it slip that he saw the ribs of a ship. Finally they ask him to keep it a secret and offer to pay him $10,000, which scares Tony. Then the harbormaster's boat comes up. Quickly the couple offer him $20,000 and half of what they find if he will just keep quiet.

As soon as he can, Tony tells Chris and Grandmother that he believes the Swallow has been found and that the couple in the motor boat are stealing things off of her. They assure Tony that the authorities will handle this.

Back at home, Tony tells everyone of his adventures, then asks if he can spend the rest of the summer with Grandmother. He knows he will not find any more treasure, but he wants to stay and sail. Instead of treasure, he would rather catch the wind, because you get to keep it.

📖 Discussion Starters 📖

Windcatcher
by Avi Wortis

1   Tony saves his paper route money to buy something special to enjoy during his vacation. Have you ever saved up money for something special? What was it? Was it worth the wait?

2   Grandmother Souza is sympathetic to Tony. When he comes back from sailing late after being lost, she buys him a watch and a compass. What other reaction might she have had?

3   What qualities make Chris a good sailing teacher?

4   When did you first become suspicious that the statue in the harbor held a clue to finding the treasure?

5   Describe the actions of the couple in the motorboat that make them suspicious.

6   Do you think it is fair for states to pass laws entitling them to treasures found off their coastal waters? Why or why not?

7   Have you ever been out on the water in a sailboat? What are the most important lessons for a beginning sailor?

8   As the model boat was quite valuable, did you expect Grandmother Souza to sell it to the antique dealer? Why or why not?

9   Once Tony finds his boat again, do you think he was wise to try to sail home in the dark, or should he have waited until morning?

10 Given what has happened in the story, do you think that Chris will be allowed to spend the whole summer instead of just three weeks with Grandmother Souza?

📖 Multidisciplinary Activities 📖

Windcatcher
by Avi Wortis

1   Design a game called "Treasure." If you are familiar with writing programs for computers, you can design your game to be played on the computer. If not, you can design it as a board game. Either way, design your game so that a player must demonstrate math proficiency in order to get a chance to dive for treasure. For example, there may be several squares on a board game marked "Dive." If, by rolling a pair of dice, a player lands on one of these spots, the player may pick a card marked "Treasure." In order to keep the treasure, however, the player must be able to correctly solve the math problem on the opposite side of the card within a specified length of time.

2   Many books have been written about treasure hunting. Check one of these books out of the library and do some browsing. When you find a treasure in which you are interested, do some research. When was this treasure found? Who found it? What led the treasure hunters to the correct spot? How valuable was the treasure? Was the treasure gold, jewels, art objects, or what? Report what you learn to your class.

3   People dive for many reasons other than treasure seeking. Careers include dive instructor, dive master, diver resort manager, diving journalist, underwater photographer, underwater cinematographer, ROV technicians (underwater Robotic Observation Vehicle), salvage divers, and underwater archaeologists. If one of these careers appeals to you, do some research on the topic. Where could you receive training? How much training is needed? Is licensing involved? Who can get a license? In an oral report, share what you learn with your class.

◆ *Bridges* ◆

📖 *Hurricanes and Storms: Repairing the Damage*
Clint Twist

📖 *Hurricane! The Rage of Hurricane Andrew*
adapted by Patricia Lantier-Sampon

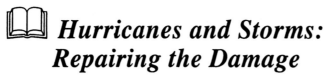 *Hurricanes and Storms: Repairing the Damage*

by Clint Twist
New York: Dillon Press, 1992. 45p.

This is one of six books from a series that looks at some of the world's natural and manmade disasters. It is illustrated with photographs, maps, and diagrams.

The text begins by pointing out that few parts of our Earth are completely free of storms. Thunderstorms can cause damage by sudden heavy rains, hailstones, and lightning. Hurricanes are much bigger than thunderstorms, often measuring 340 miles across, with winds of 200 miles an hour raging around the quiet eye of the storm. The name *hurricane* is used for a tropical revolving storm that develops in the Atlantic Ocean. In the Pacific Ocean, similar storms are called typhoons. In the Indian Ocean, they are called cyclones. The text also describes storm giants, the mid-latitude storms that occur in the middle of the Atlantic and Pacific Oceans and that can span more than 1,800 miles.

Tornadoes, or "twisters," are much smaller in diameter than hurricanes, but the winds inside a tornado can reach more than 300 mph. Other types of storms mentioned are blizzards with blowing snow, full-blown sandstorms called *khamsin* that blow for days, and smaller sandstorms called *haboobs*. The last half of the book details some of the most disastrous storms that have hit various parts of the world, weather forecasting, and climate change and weather control.

Possible Topics for Further Investigation

1 Chapter 5 of this book, "Gilbert's Story," is a diary of a tropical storm. Read it carefully and compare it to a report of a storm from a local newspaper. You will note many differences. Using just the information provided in this chapter, assume the role of a news reporter and write an article about Hurricane Gilbert. You will need to make decisions about what information to include and what to exclude. Share your article with the class.

2 Much information is available on the topic of global warming. Many scientists are convinced that this warming is not part of a natural cycle of climate but is due to the atmosphere being changed by air pollution. It has been predicted that the average temperature will increase by seven degrees Fahrenheit over the next 40 years and that polar ice caps will melt. Others believe that the danger from global warming has been exaggerated. Do some research on this topic and make your own decision about the potential danger of global warming. Share what you learn in a report to your class. Be sure to cite your sources of information.

3 This book mentions a unique approach to protecting offshore oil and gas platforms in the North Sea. Large plastic mats have been anchored to the sea bottom. The mats contains strands of buoyant plastic pieces that float upright, much like seaweed, and resist the force of waves in violent storms. Do some research on this topic and report what you learn to the class.

📖 *Hurricane!*
The Rage of Hurricane Andrew

BRIDGES

adapted by Patricia Lantier-Sampon from the *Miami Herald*
Milwaukee, WI: Gareth Stevens, 1993. 48p.

This book has simple text and dramatic color photographs. It was adapted from numerous staff reports on Hurricane Andrew that appeared in the *Miami Herald* and *El Nuevo Herald.*

Hurricane Andrew, the most devastating hurricane in U.S. history, came ashore in southern Florida on August 24, 1992. The storm destroyed 20 billion dollars worth of property in the state and demolished 25,000 homes and damaged another 50,000. Chapter 1 discusses the preparations before the hurricane hit and the evacuation of residents. It is augmented by candid shots of people buying supplies and bedding down in shelters. Chapter 2 covers the main part of the storm, which entered Florida at about 4:30 A.M. Before 5:30 A.M., the wind gauge that recorded speeds up to 164 miles an hour snapped, and there was no way to officially measure the hurricane's progress. Roofs were ripped away, furniture flew about, airplanes were destroyed, and the winds howled until about 7 A.M.

Chapter 3 details the plea for help by the survivors of the storm. Looters were stealing from devastated homes and stores, so the National Guard was called out to patrol. Power lines were down, and water was in short supply. The military set up tent cities where people could find temporary shelter. Chapter 4 describes the cleanup of the devasted area, and chapter 5 tells of hope for the future through insurance companies and federal relief.

Possible Topics for Further Investigation

1   The material for this book was adapted from reports and photos by the staff of the *Miami Herald.* Newspaper files are excellent sources of information on many topics, including storms. In many public libraries, back issues of the local newspaper or of papers such as the *New York Times* are available on microfiche. Choose a topic of interest to you, a storm or perhaps some other major event that occurred in your community. Consult with your local librarian on ways to access information about this event from the files of your local newspaper. Report to the class what you learned about using a newspaper as a source of information.

2   Researchers work out of the National Hurricane Center in Coral Gables, Florida. Find out more about this organization. When was it founded? How many people work there? Who supports this work? What sort of research do they carry out? If possible, write to a researcher at the center with your questions and report what you learn to your class.

3   Money to rebuild after a disaster is available if the business or homeowner has appropriate insurance. Invite an insurance person to visit your school to discuss the types of insurance that homeowners typically have. Have the insurance person explain what the company does when disaster strikes and an insurance adjuster inspects a home that has been burned, flooded, or destroyed by wind. Prepare questions ahead of time and be sure to thank your expert for coming.

■ *Nonfiction Connections* ■

📖 *Disastrous Hurricanes
and Tornadoes*
Max and Charlotte Alth

📖 *Hurricanes*
Sally Lee

📖 *Hurricanes and Tornadoes*
Norman Barrett

📖 *Storm Warning:
Tornadoes and Hurricanes*
Jonathan D. Kahl

📖 *Weather*
editors of *Science and Its Secrets*

📖 *Wind and Weather*
Barbara Taylor

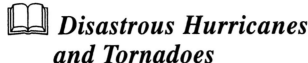

Disastrous Hurricanes and Tornadoes

by Max Alth and Charlotte Alth
New York: Franklin Watts, 1981. 66p.

Illustrated with black-and-white photographs, this book provides an excellent introduction to the disastrous effect of violent winds. It is part of a series called First Books.

The text explains that there are many different kinds of winds, all with different names. Winds are usually described by the direction from which they come. A north wind, for example, comes out of the north. People, however, differed in how they described the speed of winds until the Beaufort scale came into common use in 1805. Although somewhat rough and limited, this scale was useful. A light breeze, for example, was a 2 on the Beaufort scale—a wind moving at 4 to 7 miles per hour. A hurricane, on the other hand, had a rating of 12. In the middle of the 1800s, after dependable anemometers were developed, descriptions of wind speed became much more accurate.

Other classifications are discussed such as local, regional, and global. Local winds include sea breezes, land breezes, mountain winds, and valley winds. Regional winds include chinooks, Santa Anas, and monsoons. Global winds, caused by the temperature differences between the poles and the equator, blow constantly from the same direction and form the major wind systems of Earth. Destructive winds, such as hurricanes, typhoons, cyclones, and tornadoes, are similar in that they all rotate around a low-pressure center called an eye.

Possible Topics for Further Investigation

1 This book mentions a Greek god named Aeolus. In the legend presented, Aeolus uncovered all 12 openings in a huge cave and let the wind out when he wanted to create a storm. Read some myths and legends so that you are familiar with the form. Then write an original legend whose subject is the God of the Wind. It can be set anywhere. Make the story exciting and share it with members of your class.

2 You can make a simple aneroid barometer to share with your class. Stretch a piece of rubber from a balloon across the mouth of a milk bottle and secure it tightly with a rubber band. Take a piece of straw 10" or so in length from a broom. Glue the straw securely to the center of the rubber stretched across the milk bottle. Nail a ruler to a block of wood. Set the block near the milk bottle so that the straw touches the middle of the flat side of the upright ruler. With markers, note where the straw points on the ruler each day for a number of days. While doing this, also clip from the newspaper the barometric pressure reading given in the weather report each day. The air inside and outside the bottle exerts pressure on the rubber. When the outer air pressure decreases, the air inside the bottle pushes upward.

3 This book mentions *The Old Farmer's Almanac*, whose forecasts of the weather are based not on current scientific information but on past history. Get a copy of an almanac. For one month, write the forecast on a calendar along with the actual temperature highs and lows and notes as to whether it rained, snowed, was sunny, etc. on those days. How accurate was the *Almanac* compared to the actual weather?

Hurricanes

by Sally Lee

New York: Franklin Watts, 1993. 63p.

This is part of the First Book series and is illustrated with charts and both color and black-and-white photographs. It provides a good introduction to hurricanes.

The book begins with the story of a particularly violent hurricane, Andrew, which in August 1992 hit the Bahamas, Florida, and Louisiana. It did $30 billion worth of damage, which includes the destruction of thousands of homes in Florida. It was the most expensive natural disaster to ever hit the United States.

Hurricanes are born over warm, tropical oceans near the equator and grow until they may measure up to 500 miles across with winds of more than 150 mph. The extreme low pressure of a hurricane causes a large difference in the pressure between the storm and the surrounding area. Air rushing into the low pressure area accounts for the hurricane's high winds.

Although Hurricane Andrew was expensive, only 33 deaths were attributed to it. Other storms have caused far greater loss of life in the United States. In 1900, 6,000 people were killed in Galveston, off the Texas coast. The deadliest cyclone on record occurred in Bangladesh in 1970, when an estimated 500,000 died from the storm and the diseases that followed. The naming patterns for hurricanes and the structure of a hurricane are described, as well as how people in a hurricane's path prepare for the storm to hit.

Possible Topics for Further Investigation

1 A barometer is used to measure atmospheric pressure, which is important information in forecasting weather and determining the severity of hurricanes. Learn how to read a barometer and become familiar with what its readings indicate. When you feel familiar with one, borrow a barometer from a family member or friends and bring it to class. Make and record readings over a period of a few weeks. Next to your recordings, list the published weather reports from your newspaper. Does the barometer reading help you predict what kind of weather to expect?

2 The word *hurricane* comes either from the Spanish *huracan*, meaning "great wind," or from words used by Caribbean Indian tribes to describe evil spirits and storm gods. First do some research to find out what the elements of a legend are. Then write a legend set in the Caribbean. Have the story include an angry storm god named Huracan. Include at least three colorful illustrations. Have your teacher help you find a class of elementary students in your community that would be interested, and then read your legend to that class.

3 Hurricanes are classified using the Saffir-Simpson scale, which ranks hurricanes from 1 to 5, with categories 4 and 5 being the most severe. Look up some of the famous hurricanes that have hit the United States. Which category were they? Prepare a chart similar to the one in the book that distinguishes the various classes of hurricanes. Do some research. How long has this scale been used? How did it get its name? Share your results with your class.

Hurricanes and Tornadoes

by Norman Barrett

New York: Franklin Watts, 1989. 32p.

NONFICTION CONNECTIONS

This is a short, easy-to-ready text, illustrated with numerous color photographs. It is part of the Picture Library series of visual reference books.

The text first differentiates between hurricanes, which form over oceans and whirl around a calm area called the eye, and tornadoes, which are twisting windstorms that funnel downward from a mass of dark clouds. On a world map, readers can follow arrows that indicate the typical paths hurricanes take. A hurricane's strongest winds and heaviest rains occur in the clouds around the eye. These are called wall clouds, and the winds here may blow at speeds of up to 150 miles per hour. The eye itself, however, is fairly calm. One section of the book is devoted to a discussion of the devastation that can be caused by violent windstorms. Hurricanes can cause widespread flooding in coastal areas, down power lines, and destroy buildings.

While a hurricane can last for days, moving across the water and onto land, tornadoes are usually over in less than an hour. They form at a front between a mass of cool, dry air and a mass of warm, humid air. The speed at which a tornado moves can vary. The destruction from a tornado comes partly from the very low pressure in its eye. This tremendous difference in pressure between the inside and outside of a building may cause it to explode.

Possible Topics for Further Investigation

1. Most of us are content with calling a day calm, breezy, or very windy. Obviously, these are not very accurate classifications. This book explains the Beaufort Scale, which is a set of standard wind forces in 12 groupings. Study the Beaufort Scale shown in this book. Then prepare a pictorial representation of the scale in a large format that you can mount on a bulletin board and share with your class. You might want to listen to weather reports each night for two weeks, note the wind speed, and record it on the bulletin board using the Beaufort Scale.

2. Prepare a math game called "Hurricane" played like the traditional game SNAP. The cards will have multiplication facts and answers such as "21"; "3 x 7 = "; "14"; "2 x 7 = "; "42"; "6 x 7 = "; and so on. All cards are dealt out to two or three players who put them facedown in a stack in front of them. The dealer is first, and the players take turn in clockwise order. In turn, each player quickly turns over a card. If there is a "match," the player who first calls out "Hurricane!" takes the other player's stack and adds it to the bottom of his or her stack. The winner is the player who has the most cards.

3. Although hurricanes and tornadoes are often disasters, some humorous books have been written on the subject, such as *The Whirlys and the West Wind*. Write a humorous poem or a short story in which the wind plays amusing tricks on people. Share you work with the class.

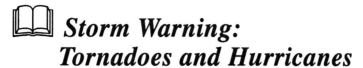

Storm Warning:
Tornadoes and Hurricanes

by Jonathan D. Kahl

Minneapolis, MN: Lerner Publications, 1993. 64p.

**NONFICTION
CONNECTIONS**

Written by a professor of atmospheric science, this is an excellent introduction to tornadoes and hurricanes. The book is illustrated with color photographs and has a good glossary of weather-related terms and a handy metric conversation chart.

Chapter 1 deals with tornadoes. The reader learns that more than 600 tornadoes touch down in the United States every year. These tornadoes usually occur between March and July and form inside cumulonimbus clouds. Three types of lifting (convective, frontal, and orographic) are discussed, as is the condensation process, which creates a special kind of energy called latent heat. The three stages of a thunderstorm are covered.

Next the book focuses on hurricanes, which are very strong storms that form over some warm parts of the North Atlantic and North Pacific oceans. Hurricanes originate near the equator where the southeast and northeast wind systems converge. While tornadoes may last only a few minutes and travel up to four miles before they dissipate, most hurricanes last about six days and may travel for many miles. Damage from hurricanes comes not only from winds but also from the large amounts of rain that fall. The book also discusses warning systems, storm safety tips, and gives information about famous tornadoes and hurricanes and the damage they have caused.

Possible Topics for Further Investigation

1 On pages 34 and 35, the text explains how to make a tornado. To perform this experiment for your class, you will use two empty one-liter pop bottles, their caps, and a balloon. Fill one bottle two-thirds full of water. Use a large nail to punch a 1/4" hole in the center of each bottle cap. Cut the round end off the balloon and throw it away. Fit the neck of the remaining balloon piece over the neck of the empty bottle. Turn this bottle upside down, and fit the cut end of the balloon over the neck of the bottle with water in it. Stand the empty bottle upright on top of the bottle with water. Get them as close together as possible and make a tight fit. Then quickly turn the bottles over so that the bottle with water is on top. With one hand, hold the necks of the two bottles together. With the other hand, twirl the bottle with water in a circular motion, until water begins to drain through the hole. As the water drains, you will see a vortex.

2 Included in the book is a metric conversion chart. Use this information to write a series of problems for your classmates in which they convert acres to hectares, square miles to square kilometers, feet to meters, yards to meters, and inches to centimeters.

3 NEXRAD, or Next Generation Weather Radar, is a system of Doppler radar equipment operated by the National Weather Service. Do some research to learn more about NEXRAD and how it works. Report what you learn to your class.

 *Weather*

by the editors of *Science and Its Secrets*
Milwaukee, WI: Raintree, 1988. 64p.

This is a large-format book illustrated with color photographs. It provides an introduction to various aspects of weather, including seasons, climate, and unpredictable weather. Although this book is being included in the section on "Winds," it could be used as a resource in any one of the four sections of this book.

The sections of particular interest to this unit of study are "Unpredictable Weather" and the portion dealing with predicting and the discussion of how meteorological information is obtained, how it is used, and the importance of weather reports. The reader learns that winds are created by temperature differences that exist on the surface of the Earth. When warm air rises, it leaves an empty space where it once was, and cooler air moves in to fill that space. The movement of air from one space to another is what causes wind.

Heavy winds can cause damage in a variety of ways. There is an excellent photograph of an Oklahoma tornado and a description of tornadoes in general. A large amount of energy is concentrated into a very small space; the winds inside a tornado can rotate at more than 186 miles per hour. Short description are also provided of winds that turn snowstorms into blizzards, and cyclones where winds spiral inward.

Possible Topics for Further Investigation

1 One weather instrument that is of particular importance in this section is the anemometer, which measures wind speed. Anemometers are relatively common. Try to locate one in your community. If your school has a weather station, an anemometer will certainly be included. Learn how it works. Make a detailed diagram of the parts of an anemometer and explain its workings to your class.

2 This book contains a lot of information that could be used in constructing some interesting math problems for your classmates to solve. For example, you might ask, "If 11 seconds elapse between seeing a flash of lightning and hearing the sound of thunder, what would you estimate is the distance to the point where the lightning is produced?" You will have to provide such information as that the speed of sound is 1,115 feet per second. Prepare a few questions for your classmates.

3 The old saying goes that everyone complains about the weather, but no one does anything about it. Actually, people are beginning to investigate ways to change the weather. Ask your media specialist to help you locate information about a project called Stormfury that is mentioned in this book. It aims to diminish the intensity of hurricanes by a very complicated scheme to modify the eye of the cyclone. Share what you learn with your classmates. In your research, did you come up with other projects to modify weather, such as seeding clouds to produce rain or shooting clouds that look as if they would produce hail?

Wind and Weather

by Barbara Taylor

New York: Franklin Watts, 1991. 32p.

This is a large-format, easy-to-read book, illustrated with color pictures. It is part of a series of books called Science Starters and includes some step-by-step science investigations.

The book is an introduction to the effect of wind on people and the environment. It is divided into seven sections: air on the move, using the wind, environment, plants, air pressure, measuring weather, and pollution.

The first section of this book points out ways in which the powerful force of the wind is used for such things as sailing and electrical power generation. In the section on environment, pictures show wind shaping sand dunes and the effect of sand and wind blowing against rock formations. It is pointed out that plants depend on wind to scatter their seeds and pollen.

The section on predicting weather discusses such things as highs and lows and how these appear on weather charts; barometric pressure; the Beaufort scale for measuring wind; making a barometer and an anemometer; and using such information to make a weather forecast. The section of this book that deals with pollution in the air suggests that a lot of air pollution is caused by invisible gases such as carbon dioxide from power stations and cars and from the burning of rainforests. The book concludes with ideas for additional projects such as making a windmill, a weather book, and a wind speed box.

Possible Topics for Further Investigation

1   Page 7 of this book shows a field of modern windmills that are used to turn wind power into electricity. The advantage of this type of power generation is that no gas or oil is used, so windmills do not pollute the air and use up scarce energy sources. Such generators, however, will work only in places where strong winds blow most of the time. Research this energy source. Where is the nearest "windmill field"? Where are they found throughout the world? Are they proving to be effective for generating electricity? What are their major assets and drawbacks? Report what you learn to the class.

2   Page 15 of the text gives simple directions, clarified by an illustration, showing you how to make a simple barometer to measure the changes in air pressure. Following these directions, make a barometer and take it to your classroom. Set regular times of the day to read and record the measurements on your barometer. Post your readings. Next to them, post the readings from a standard barometer that you also read or the barometric pressure reported in your newspaper or on your television weather report. Does your homemade barometer seem to be accurate? Does it help you predict changes in the weather?

3   Page 21 of the text gives directions for making a simple anemometer to measure how fast the wind is blowing. Follow these directions. Find a place at home or at school where you can set up your anemometer. Record your results over several weeks and present your findings in an oral report using charts you prepare.

Part V

Additional Resources and Linkages

📖 Questions That Link Various 📖 Fiction Books

1 Evan in *Canyons Beyond the Sky* and Matthew Morgan in *Frozen Fire* have much in common. Both boys have fathers who are geologists and who are away from home a good deal in their search for metals, bones, or artifacts. Neither father has much time for his son. Discuss ways in which these pairs of characters are similar and different.

2 In *Frozen Fire*, Matt's Eskimo friend, Kayak, makes a long and difficult journey with him through the frozen wasteland. In *Life in the Desert*, Rebecca makes a sort of mind journey with O. Z. through the desert of O. Z.'s mind. What traits do these two friends share? In what ways are they different?

3 In *Dustland*, Dorian's mother, Mrs. Jefferson, prepares the four children to go on a journey into the future that she herself does not take. In *Dogsong*, Oogruk prepares Russel to go on a journey into a past way of life. How are the roles of Mrs. Jefferson and Oogruk alike and different?

4 Princess Antia in *Sandwriter* is an orphan. Shiva from *Shiva: An Adventure of the Ice Age* is also an orphan. In what ways are Antia and Shiva alike, and in what ways are they different?

5 In *Ice Warrior*, Rob moves into an environment with which he's totally unfamiliar. In *Canyons Beyond the Sky*, Evan moves into a similar situation. Both boys end up being successful in their new setting. Are the factors that contribute to each boy's success similar or different?

6 The relationship between Lewis and Rachel in *After the Rain* grows slowly, as does the relationship between O. Z. and Rebecca in *Life in the Desert*. Five years from the end of each story, do you think either of these couples will still be close? Why or why not?

7 Grandpa Izzy from *After the Rain* and Oogruk from *Dogsong* both admire men who work hard and can do things with their hands. Although they lived in different times and places, if these two men were thrown together, do you think they would be friends or enemies? Why?

8 In *Dustland*, one of the major characters is called Justice. The baby in *The Day It Rained Forever* is called Hope. Why is each of these names especially appropriate?

9 Matthew's dad in *Frozen Fire* could easily have perished in the frozen land where the helicopter went down. Christina's mother in *The Day It Rained Forever* could easily have drowned when the dam broke. Which of these two situations seemed most frightening to you and why?

10 In *Dustland*, Justice worries about her brother. In *No Way Out*, Amy worries about her brother. Both brothers survive terrible ordeals. How are the fears of Justice and Amy alike, and how are they different?

11 In *Frozen Fire*, Matt and Kayak quickly develop a close friendship. In *No Way Out*, Ben and Clyde quickly become buddies. What circumstances caused both friendships to develop so quickly?

12 In *Canyons Beyond the Sky*, Matthew is struck by the beauty of the canyons and also learns to fear them. In *No Way Out*, Amy is similarly struck by the beauty of the Narrows and learns to fear them. Why do you think Matthew is looking forward to returning to the canyons, but Amy plans never to return to the Narrows?

13 O. Z. in *Life in the Desert* tries to commit suicide. Neale in *No Way Out* has tried to commit suicide. Do you think their reasons for trying to end their lives were similar?

14 Princess Antia survives a terrible desert storm in *Sandwriter*. Amy survives a flood in *No Way Out*. If you had to choose trying to survive a desert storm or a flash flood, which would you choose and why?

15 In *Frozen Fire*, the "wild man" has torn all the hands off his watches. In *The Rain Catchers*, Grandmother has torn all the hands off her clocks. Are the reasons for these actions similar or not? Discuss.

16 Grayling falls under the spell of Dancer in *The Rain Catchers*. Princess Antia is under the spell of Eskoril in *Sandwriter*. In what ways are Dancer and Eskoril alike, and in what ways are they different?

17 In *Windcatcher*, Tony wants to learn how to sail. In *Ice Warrior*, Rob wants to learn how to sail on the ice. Both succeed. What different challenges did they face?

18 What traits do Oogruk from *Dogsong* and Tom from *Devil Storm* share? How are they different?

19 Two friends survive a night of tornadoes in *Night of the Twisters*. Two friends survive an ice adventure in *Frozen Fire*. Which of these ordeals do you think was worse, and why?

20 Babies play significant roles in *Devil Storm* and in *The Day It Rained Forever*. Both stories also feature the recent death of a child. In what ways do the mothers in these stories react similarly and differently?

21 Grandmother in *The Rain Catchers* and Grandfather in *After the Rain* are very different types of people, but they have some similarities. What are these?

22 Ivy Ruckman wrote both *No Way Out* and *Night of the Twisters*. Which of these two books did you enjoy the most, and why?

23 Shiva from *Shiva: An Adventure of the Ice Age* and Alyssa from *Silent Storm* are strong young women. Besides their strength and stamina, what other similarities do you find?

24 Princess Antia in *Sandwriter* and Grayling in *The Rain Catchers* might be called romantics. How are these two young women alike, and how are they different?

25 Necklaces play roles in *The Silent Storm* and in *Devil Storm*. In both cases they serve as reminders of the past. Which is the more effective symbol and why?

26 If Tony from *Windcatcher*, instead of Rob from *Ice Warrior*, had been relocated to Minnesota, do you think Tony would have had the same problems that Rob had? Why or why not?

27 Russel from *Dogsong* and Ty from *Silent Storm* both had alcoholic fathers. How does alcoholism affect each of the stories?

28 Shiva from *Shiva: An Adventure of the Ice Age* and Stacey from *Night of the Twisters* are both resourceful people. Cite instances from each story to demonstrate this trait.

29 The grandmothers in *Windcatcher* and in *After the Rain* have profound influences on their grandchildren. As adults, will Tony or Grayling show the most effect from their interactions with their grandmothers? Why?

📖 Using Picture Books with 📖 Middle-Grade Readers

There are countless activities using picture books through which teachers can involve middle-grade readers. The ones listed below are but a few.

Snow Toward Evening: A Year in River Valley. Nature poems selected by Josette Frank. Paintings by Tony Johnson. New York: Dial Books, 1990.

This work contains 13 poems, one for each month of the year, plus one titled "A New Year." The illustrations are quite beautiful. A teacher might use this book to encourage students to write original poetry about weather. "Mountain Wind" and "Wind Has Shaken Autumn Down" would be particularly popular while studying part IV.

Thunder Cake by Patricia Polacco. New York: Philomel Books, 1990.

Thunder Cake would be an excellent book for a middle-grade student to read to a kindergarten or first-grade class. It describes the frightening noise of thunder before a heavy rainstorm. The book concludes with a recipe for thunder cake. If adults are willing to help, and if cooking facilities are available, this might make an excellent primary-grade cooking project. This would be a particularly appropriate activity while studying part III.

Owl Moon by Jane Yolen. New York: Philomel Books, 1987.

This is one of many picture books that might be used with part I. Knowing what conditions are right for animal observations, accurately imitating bird calls, and recognizing tracks of different creatures in the snow will intrigue some students. Some might want to look into tracking in the snow, while others might want to study the habits and calls of various snow birds.

Drylongso by Virginia Hamilton. San Diego, CA: Harcourt Brace Jovanovich, 1992.

This 54-page picture book would enrich part II. Many of the books in the nonfiction connections in part II deal with the Dust Bowl. This book depicts in words and pictures the drama of one quartet who face a wall of black dust that envelopes their home and farm. It also shows the use of a dowser, about which some middle-grade students might be curious and want to investigate further.

📖 Fiction Titles 📖

Snow, Hail, and Ice

Dekkers, Midas. *Arctic Adventure.* New York: Franklin Watts; Orchard Books, 1987. 165p.

Hill, Kirkpatrick. *Winter Camp.* New York: Margaret K. McElderry Books, 1993. 185p.

Houston, James A. *Drifting Snow: An Arctic Search.* New York: Margaret K. McElderry Books, 1992. 150p.

Lutzeier, Elizabeth. *The Coldest Winter.* New York: Holiday House, 1991. 153p.

Murphy, Claire Rudolf. *To the Summit.* New York: Lodestar, 1992. 156p.

Roper, Robert. *In Caverns of Blue Ice.* Boston: Little, Brown, 1991. 188p.

Drought, Dust, and Dunes

Brittain, Bill. *Dr. Dredd's Wagon of Wonders.* New York: Harper & Row, 1987. 179p.

MacLachlan, Patricia. *Skylark.* New York: HarperCollins, 1994. 86p.

Rossiter, Phyllis. *Moxie.* New York: Four Winds Press; Maxwell Macmillan, 1990. 185p.

Russell, Sharman. *The Humpbacked Fluteplayer.* New York: Alfred A. Knopf, 1994. 179p.

Schaefer, Jack. *Old Ramon.* New York: Walker, 1993. 102p.

Service, Pamela F. *Vision Quest.* New York: Atheneum, 1989. 136p.

Clouds, Rain, and Floods

Byars, Betsy Cromer. *A Blossom Promise.* New York: Delacorte Press, 1987. 145p.

Curry, Jane Louise. *The Great Flood Mystery.* New York: Atheneum, 1985. 171p.

Gordon, Sheila. *Waiting for the Rain: A Novel of South Africa.* New York: Orchard Books, 1987. 214p.

L'Engle, Madeleine. *Many Waters.* New York: Farrar, Straus & Giroux, 1986. 310p.

Paulsen, Gary. *The Voyage of the Frog.* New York: Orchard Books, 1989. 142p.

Skurzynski, Gloria. *Trapped in the Slickrock Canyon.* New York: Lothrop, Lee & Shepard, 1984. 123p.

Winds:
Hurricanes, Tornadoes, and Typhoons

Fox, Paula. *Western Wind: A Novel.* New York: Orchard Books, 1993. 201p.

Lasky, Kathryn. *A Voice in the Wind.* San Diego, CA: Harcourt Brace, 1993. 256p.

Maky, Margaret. *The Blood-and-Thunder Adventure on Hurricane Peak.* New York: Margaret K. McElderry Books, 1989. 132p.

Milton, Hilary H. *Tornado!* New York: Franklin Watts, 1983. 147p.

Pendergraft, Patricia. *Hear the Wind Blow.* New York: Philomel Books, 1988. 208p.

Watson, J. B. *The Hurricane.* New York: Grosset & Dunlap, 1994. 152p.

📖 Nonfiction Titles 📖

Snow, Hail, and Ice

Evans, Jeremy. *Skiing.* New York: Crestwood House, 1992. 48p.

Gaff, Jackie. *Skiing and Snow Sports.* New York: Warwick Press, 1989. 40p.

Guthrie, Robert W. *Hot Dogging and Snowboarding.* Mankato, MN: Capstone Press, 1992. 48p.

Jacobs, Leland B. *Just Around the Corner: Poems About the Seasons.* New York: Henry Holt, 1993. 32p.

Otfinoski, Steven. *Blizzards.* New York: Twenty-First Century Books, 1994. 64p.

Tibbitts, Alison. *Snow Leopards.* Mankato, MN: Capstone Press, 1992. 32p.

Drought, Dust, and Dunes

Bowers, Janice Emily. *Seasons of the Wind: A Naturalist's Look at the Plant Life of Southwestern Sand Dunes.* Flagstaff, AZ: Northland Press, 1986. 156p.

Dolan, Edward F. *Drought: The Past, Present and Future Enemy.* New York: Franklin Watts, 1990. 144 p.

Knapp, Brian J. *Drought.* Austin, TX: Raintree/Steck-Vaughn, 1990. 48p.

Peissel, Michel. *Dangerous Natural Phenomena.* New York: Chelsea House, 1993. 111p.

Walker, Jane. *Famine, Drought and Plagues.* New York: Gloucester Press, 1992. 32p.

Warren, Scott S. *Cities in the Sand: The Ancient Civilizations of the Southwest.* San Francisco, CA: Chronicle Books, 1992. 55p.

Clouds, Rain, and Floods

Ganeri, Anita. *The Weather.* New York: Franklin Watts, 1993. 32p.

Gibbons, Gail. *Nature's Green Umbrella: Tropical Rain Forests.* New York: Morrow Junior Books, 1994. 30p.

Gutnik, Martin J. *Experiments That Explore Acid Rain.* Brookfield, CT: Millbrook Press, 1992. 72p.

Liptak, Karen. *Inside Biosphere 2: The Rainforest.* Oracle, AZ: Biosphere Press, 1994. 64p.

Macdonald, Fiona. *Rain Forest.* Austin, TX: Raintree/Steck-Vaughn, 1994. 32p.

Palmer, Joy. *Rain.* Austin, TX: Raintree/Steck-Vaughn, 1993. 32p.

Winds:
Hurricanes, Tornadoes, and Typhoons

Berger, Melvin. *A Look at Weather and How It Changes.* Nashville, TN: Ideals Children's Books, 1993. 48p.

Carless, Jennifer. *Renewable Energy: A Concise Guide to Green Alternatives.* New York: Walker, 1993. 168p.

Cooper, Jason. *Wind.* Vero Beach, FL: Rourke Corporation, 1992. 24p.

Cross, Mike. *Wind Power.* New York: Gloucester Press, 1985. 31p.

Lampton, Christopher. *Blizzard.* Brookfield, CT: Millbrook Press, 1991. 64p.

Sauvain, Philip Arthur. *Wind and Water Power.* Lexington, MA: Schoolhouse Press, 1988. 48p.

Author-Title Index

155

About the Author

Dr. Phyllis J. Perry has taught in California, New Jersey, and Colorado, from second grade to graduate school. She has been a teacher, a curriculum specialist, a director of talented-and-gifted education, a principal, and a university supervisor of student teachers. Throughout, she has had a strong interest in a multidisciplinary approach to education.

Dr. Perry is the author of 22 books for children and adults, including *A Teacher's Science Companion* (TAB Books/McGraw-Hill, 1994), *Colorado History* (Hi Willow Press, 1994), *The Fiddlehoppers* (Franklin Watts, 1995), and *Getting Started in Science Fairs* (TAB Books/McGraw-Hill, 1995). She also writes plays, poetry, articles, and fiction for a variety of children's magazines.